THE DAY OF THE LORD DRAWS CLOSER

THE DAY OF THE LORD DRAWS CLOSER

by

Paul Flynn

Creative Christian Publishing

The Day of the Lord Draws Closer
by Paul Flynn

Published 2020 by
Creative Christian Publishing
The Grange, London SW19
writerscheckup@msn.com

ISBN 978-0-9539179-9-0

Copyright 2020 © by Paul Flynn

All rights reserved. The author guarantees that all contents are original and do not infringe the rights of any other person or work.

Bible quotations are taken from the New Jerusalem Version, Copyright © 1985 by Darton, Longman & Todd Ltd., and from the King James Version.

Other works by Paul Flynn:

M.E./Chronic Fatigue Syndrome, A Short Handbook (2010)
The Arrow of Elisha (2013)
Mary and the Prayer Patterns in the Song of Songs (2014)
The Blessing and the Curse of Johnny Cash (2015)
Elijah the Tishbite (2016)
This is My Body, The Eucharist, the Creation, and the Coming World Order (2017)
Under the Apple Tree, A Life of Mary (2018)
Dormition? (2019)

'This is the day whereof I have spoken.'

— Ezekiel 39:8

CONTENTS

PREFACE	10
INTRODUCTION	12
EZEKIEL 38,39	23
ESTHER	53
THE PSALMS	56
WISDOM	67
ISAIAH	74
JEREMIAH	89
OTHER TEXTS IN EZEKIEL	96
DANIEL	99
JOEL	108

HABAKKUK	116
ZEPHANIAH	133
HAGGAI AND THE EUCHARIST	146
ZECHARIAH	152
THE GOSPELS	162
2 THESSALONIANS	179
REVELATION – The Architecture	190
REVELATION 11 – The Two Witnesses	216
REVELATION 12	228
REVELATION 13	248
REVELATION 17 & 18	270
REVELATION 19 & 20	285

SIGNS OF THE TIMES	290
THE DIFFERENCE	301
WHAT WILL IT LOOK LIKE AFTER THE DAY?	311

PREFACE

The many prophecies of the Day of the Lord are scattered throughout Scripture. They run through the prophets, and the psalms, and the gospels; they are present in the Wisdom books and in the apostolic Letters; the architecture of the Book or Revelation is designed around seven separate descriptions of the Day of the Lord.

When we draw all of these prophecies together, which is my purpose in this work, we see that they are all consistent with each other; they add to each other's detail but they never contradict each other; they are insistently physical; they do not allow us to read them as allegory or symbol or anything else but what they actually describe; they make it clear that the impact of the terrifying Day will be centered in Israel and Jerusalem but will extend to the entire world; they make it repeatedly and wholly clear that the one who will appear as the Warrior-Messiah on the Day of the Lord is Christ the King in his humanity; the outcome of the terrifying events of the Day will be the knowledge, throughout the earth and beginning with Israel, that the only God and Savior of all the peoples of all the nations on earth is the God who reveals himself in Christ; this knowledge will not depart from the earth again from the time of the Day to the time of the close of the age.

The times we are living through might look chaotic and threatening, but in the prophecies of the Day of the Lord God tells us that he knows what he is doing. Everything is moving toward a historic climax. The events will be terrifying, but they need not take us by surprise, and we have the assurance from God himself that what will emerge from the fearsome events will be a world cleansed and undeceived, and a Church made ready for its time of greatest glory.

INTRODUCTION

Two provocations figure constantly in Scripture as the triggers prompting the terrifying appearance of the Lord when his Day comes. Both will happen in the immediate run up to the Day of the Lord. The attack against Jerusalem is one of them. The other is the abolition of the daily sacrifice and the installation in its place of the abomination of desolation.

It is very clear from this that the Lord is highly sensitive about both Jerusalem and the Eucharist. An assault against either is an attack against the plans of God which are most intimate to his heart. It is impossible to understand what is happening in the biblical descriptions of the Day of the Lord without understanding these two things, God's sensitivity about Jerusalem and his sensitivity about the Eucharist.

The spirit of Antichrist works might and main with all his hosts of wicked angels to bring down God's holy people. He outrages God to his face with the most horrible blasphemies. He corrupts the faith of countless millions. The patience of God still holds out.

But when the spirit of Antichrist leads his vast armies to take over Jerusalem for his own filthy purposes, and when he brings the daily sacrifice to an end and replaces it with a fake version of the Eucharist designed to honor himself rather than God, that is when the patience of God is exhausted. That is when the terrifying events of the Day of the Lord are about to begin.

To understand this we need to understand that the Incarnation of Christ is at the center of the designs of God's heart. The doctrine of the Incarnation of Christ is not just one doctrine among many. It is the doctrine which our enemy the devil works most furiously against. We have no conception of how determined our enemy the devil, the Antichrist, is to rob us of our belief in the Incarnation of Christ.

Why is this? Why is our enemy the devil so infuriated by the Incarnation of Christ that he devotes all his energies and all his legions of wicked angels to his warfare against it?

If he can discredit the doctrine of the Incarnation the whole of Christian doctrine comes down with it. If the Son of God did not really become incarnate, then he didn't really die, and so we are not saved from our sins. And if he didn't die, he didn't rise from the dead, and so our faith is in vain.

This is all true, and the Church in its liturgies subordinates the doctrine of the Incarnation to the doctrine of the death and Resurrection of Christ. Easter, not Christmas is the central celebration of the Church calendar, because if Christ only became incarnate we would not be saved from our bondage to the devil through sin. Our salvation came about through the Cross and Resurrection of Our Lord.

And yet, though it is not treated as the principal doctrine, there is something about the Incarnation that is uniquely infuriating to the devil and his wicked angels. The very idea of God taking on himself the form of an embodied spirit and not the form of a pure spirit is most abhorrent to Lucifer's pride.

We will discuss this further in the chapter of this book about Revelation 12, so I will be brief here. In the beginning, in his eternity, before he brought any creature into existence, God had a desire born out of his overflowing love. The life God enjoys in the love of the three Persons of the Trinity is infinitely satisfactory to him. God needs nothing else.

But out of his infinite generosity God sees the possibility of something more. You cannot add to infinity. God doesn't need anything more, but love is gratuitous. It gives. It never ceases to overflow. From his eternity God saw the possibility of making creatures with a nature like his own, a spiritual nature, creatures with whom he could share his life.

So God created the angels, pure spirits like himself who delighted in sharing his life by praising and worshiping him and so receiving him spiritually, in all the fullness of their created spiritual capacity to receive him. God delighted in his angels and his angels delighted in him.

But with God there is always more. Greatly as he delighted in his angels, God wanted to make a creature to whom he could give himself without restriction, not only in all the fullness of the creature's capacity to receive him spiritually, but in all the fullness of his own Godhead. How could he do this? If he couldn't do it with pure spirits, creatures with a nature like his own, surely he couldn't do it at all?

No, you can't shorten the hand of God. God wanted to do it, and he thought of a way. The way was Christ. He couldn't do it by taking on the nature of a spirit. He already existed as a spirit. But he could do it by taking a body. He could do it by becoming an embodied spirit, or an enspirited body. You can say it either way.

An embodied spirit, Christ, is God in all his fullness. 'For in him all the fullness of the Godhead is pleased to dwell bodily' (Colossians 2:9). And embodied spirits – we, his church – can receive him in all the fullness of his Godhead precisely because of this, his Incarnation. What we could never have done spiritually, we can do bodily. Through the Eucharist, and in no other way, we can fulfill the eternal desire of God, to give himself to his beloved creature not only in all the fullness of the creature's capacity to receive him spiritually, but in all the fullness of his own Godhead, bodily.

This is the reason for the creation of the material universe. 'Sacrifice and offering you desired not, but you have prepared for me a body' (Hebrews 10:5).

The Incarnation of Christ is the reason for the creation of the material universe. Only by taking a body could God fulfill the most intimate desires of his heart. 'For verily he took not on him the nature of angels, but he took on him the seed of Abraham' (Hebrews 2:16).

When the angels learned of the plan of God, they were delighted with it, and were ready and eager to serve in the kingdom which God would establish under Christ. Not all of them were delighted with the plans of God, however. What to God was most delightful, to his most gifted but proud creature was so utterly infuriating, so utterly humiliating that he rose up against it and persuaded a third of the angels of God to join his rebellion.

The idea that God would create a race of embodied spirits was hateful enough to Satan. An embodied spirit, being naturally inferior to a pure spirit, was to the devil's haughty spirit an idea so contemptible that he couldn't bear to think of it. But that God should himself choose to take on the inferior form, thus exalting the inferior form above the angelic form, and then require Lucifer himself, the greatest of all God's creatures, to serve in the kingdom ruled over by the embodied Son of God, this was so outrageous to the proud spirit that he conceived a furious desire to make war with it, and he and his wicked followers have been making relentless war on it ever since.

This, briefly, is the reason the spirit of Antichrist never stops in his warfare against Jerusalem, the capital city of Christ's earthly family, and against the daily sacrifice, the Mass, the Eucharist. And this is why, when the Day of the Lord strikes, as prophesied so many times in Scripture, it will be in response to the Antichrist's climactic twin attacks against Jerusalem and against the Eucharist.

When we see how insistent are our Lord's warnings about the Day of the Lord, how frequently and how graphically it is described in the Bible, we realize that he really wants us to know about the events he describes. Even though they are far in the future, and even though we are never told when they will take place, he really wants us to know about them.

Why is this? Why does he want us to know in detail about events that are, or at least were when he told us of them, to happen far in the future?

Nowhere is this question more clearly answered than in the Book of Habakkuk. We will discuss this Book in a later chapter so, again, I will be brief here. The Book of Habakkuk opens with the prophet wrestling with the question we all wrestle with. Why does God leave his people at the mercy of their wicked enemies? Why does he not take immediate action to bring the wicked to book now?

God answers Habakkuk. He tells him that he is not standing idly by at all. His Day will come, and the vision of his Day will come. Wait for it, even if it delays awhile, because come the vision certainly will.

In the lifetime of Habakkuk the Day of the Lord was thousands of years in the future, yet the Lord told Habakkuk to wait for the vision of the Day, as if the vision would in some way be as effective as the Day itself. He told him to write the vision down. He wanted the vision to be recorded in Scripture for all to see.

God wants everyone to experience the Day of the Lord. When it happens, it will be seen by everyone throughout the world. It will also be seen by all succeeding generations, for whom it will be recorded. And it will be seen by all generations coming into the world before the Day of the Lord because they will have access to the visions of the prophets as recorded in Scripture.

When Habakkuk had his vision of the Day of the Lord he was shaken to his depths by it. It almost overwhelmed him, so deeply disturbed was he by it, but in the end he came through the trial stronger, better, wiser for having had the vision of the Day.

And that is what should happen to us all. We cannot enter into the prophetic visions of the Day of the Lord as dispassionate observers. Coming face to face with the Day of the Lord is not an academic activity. It is deeply disturbing. It forces us to confront our complacency, our lack of faith. It forces us to recognize our two mindedness. It forces us to face the choice we have always been faced with though we perhaps didn't yet realize it: the choice between Christ and Antichrist.

If we have not yet made a clear choice for Christ, the vision of the Day will take us by surprise and we will not be able to face the trial. 'He whose heart is not upright will succumb' (Habakkuk 2:4). He who is still undecided whether he belongs to Christ or Antichrist will be overwhelmed by the vision.

'But the just will live by faith' (Habakkuk 2:4). The one who is true to his baptismal vows, who places all his trust in Christ and utterly renounces Antichrist, will come through the vision of the Day of the Lord stronger and better for having seen it.

'Purify your hearts, ye double minded' (James 4:8). This is the purpose of the many prophecies in the Bible about the Day of the Lord. This is the reason the events of the Day are described so forcefully, so graphically that it is as if we are actually witnessing them. The purpose of the prophecies about the Day is to prepare us, to purify our hearts so that we deal with the terrifying events before they are upon us.

In the pages following we will, so far as I can recognize them, run through all the passages in Scripture which describe the Day of the Lord. We will try to explore the extent and the power of the biblical prophecies about the Day; we will try to relate them to the events of our time to see how these events are moving toward the Day; and we will see how they confirm and add to each other to build up as complete a picture of the Day as possible.

EZEKIEL 38 & 39

These two prophetic chapters are central to any account of the Day of the Lord. We will return to them frequently in the later chapters of this work. Much detail is missing in Ezekiel 38 and 39; much remains to be said; but what is said in Ezekiel 38 and 39 is so compelling, so graphic, so real, that it can be taken as something like the central account of the Day of the Lord in all of Scripture. We will now go through each passage in turn to see what we can glean from it.

The word of the Lord came to me, saying, Son of man, set your face against Gog, in the land of Magog, the chief prince of Meshech and Tubal, and prophesy against him. Say, 'The Lord God says this, Behold, I am against you Gog, the chief prince of Meshech and Tubal. - Ezekiel 38:1-3

This introduction to the prophecy tells us that the ruler against whom Ezekiel is to prophesy is the ruler of a place which corresponds to the greater part of modern Turkey. This ruler is an enemy of God. Whatever he is doing, whatever plans he is hatching, are hostile to God and to God's people. From the length of the introduction it is clear that a very major prophecy is about to be uttered.

I will turn you about, and put hooks in your jaws, and I will bring you out with your whole army, horses, and horsemen, all of them thoroughly equipped, a vast array armed with shields and bucklers, and all of them handling swords. – Ezekiel 38:4.

The ruler, Gog, may think he is acting by his own authority and on no one's prompting but his own; yet the text describes him as putty in the hand of Yahweh, who will put hooks in his jaws as one controls an animal, and will bring him out as one brings a horse out of its stable.

Gog will be at the head of a vast army, on so great a military expedition, with such great strength in the number of his troops that no one could imagine that he might be on a doomed venture. No one would dare suggest that so great a force could be marching out to its own defeat. Yet we know from the outset that the God of Israel is in total control of the entire project.

Gog will not be leading his own troops alone. He will be leading them at the head of an international coalition of armies. The combined force of these armies is such that there is nothing in military history to compare with it.

Persia, Cush and Put are with them, all with buckler and helmet; Gomer and all his troops, Beth Togarmah in the far north and all its troops, and many nations with you. Be ready, be well prepared, you and all your troops and the other troops rallying to you, and hold yourself at my service. - Ezekiel 38:5-7

The nations whose armies will join Gog in this expedition will include Persia (modern Iran); Cush, (Sudan and parts of Somalia); Put (modern Libya); Gomer and Beth Togarmah, (parts of modern Turkey).

The 'many nations with you' are not named here, but at least some of them are named elsewhere in the prophecies about the Day of the Lord. As we will see later, they include Egypt, Syria, Tyre and Sidon (in modern Lebanon), and the territory of the Philistines.

All of these nations coming against Israel are currently Muslim majority areas. Whether they will still be Muslim majority areas when the Day arrives is unknown. They will be sufficiently hostile to Israel for their armies to join in a war against her.

'Hold yourself at my service,' the Lord tells Gog, reminding us that it is he, Yahweh of Israel, who is in complete control of all the action, and that his enemies act in his service even while they are seeking to make war against him and his people.

Many days will pass before you are given orders; in the final years you will march on this country, whose inhabitants will have been living in confidence, remote from other peoples, since they escaped the sword and were gathered in from many nations, here in the long deserted mountains of Israel. Like a storm you will approach, you will advance and cover the land like a cloud, you, all your troops, and many nations with you.

- Ezekiel 38:8,9

We are dealing with an end times prophecy. It will happen in the final days, after many years, when the people of Israel, long dispersed among all the nations on earth, will at last have returned to their land and will be dwelling at peace, not suspecting anything of the plots being hatched against them.

Israel's enemies are being held up God's sleeve, so to speak, in the long centuries leading up to the Day on which he will call them to begin their attack, the Day on which his glory will become manifest to his people Israel and to all the peoples of the earth. They will advance like a storm, and cover the country like a cloud.

Thus says the Lord God: That Day, a thing will come into your mind and you will think an evil thought; and you will say, I will go up to the land of unwanted villages; I will go to those who are at rest, who dwell safely, all of them dwelling without walls, and having neither bars nor gates. You will come to plunder and loot, and turn your hand against the desolate places that are now inhabited, and against the people that are gathered out of the nations, who have got cattle and goods and dwell in the midst of the land. Sheba and Dedan, the merchants and all the magnates of Tarshish will ask you: Have you come for plunder? Are you massing your troops with a view to looting? To make off with gold and silver, seize cattle and goods, and come away with a great spoil? - Ezekiel 38:10-13

The question raised by the peoples of Arabia and other trading nations highlight the contrast between the sleepy attitudes dominating the complacent world immediately before the Day, and the cataclysm that is about to strike. Their minds are focused only on the coming commercial opportunities.

Like the vast hordes coming against Israel, they have no clue that the Almighty is the defender of his people, that his people are the apple of his eye, that the Messiah is about to engage, and that they are on the wrong side in the contest. It is a very serious mistake to come against the people of Israel. To come against his people is to come against God himself. And yet those who are led by the spirit of Antichrist, the spirit of evil, will dare to do it.

So, son of man, prophesy. Say to Gog, The Lord Yahweh says this, Is it not true that you will set out at a time when my people Israel is living secure? You will come from your place in the north parts, you and many nations with you, all of them riding upon horses, a great company and a mighty army. And you will come against my people Israel. You will be like a cloud covering the land. In the final days, I myself will bring you to attack my country, so that the nations will know who I am, when I display my holiness to them by means of you, Gog. - Ezekiel 38:14-16

The repetitions here emphasize that it is the God of Israel who will be in control of the entire expedition; that it will happen in the end times, 'the final days;' that Gog will attack when Israel least expects it; that he will be joined by an international coalition of unprecedented force; that the armies following him will cover the land like a cloud.

This is the first passage in which God speaks of his purpose in arranging the mass invasion of Israel. Up to this point we have only been told that the Lord will 'put hooks in his jaws,' will provide the circumstances in which Gog will be motivated to lead his forces against Israel. Now God begins to tell us why: he is about to reveal to the nations who he is. He is about to display his holiness to all the nations on the earth by means of the enemies of Israel acting under the leadership of Gog, the chief prince of Meshech and Tubal.

The nations of the earth are about to learn that salvation is indeed of the Jews; that Yahweh of Israel has indeed come among his people in flesh and blood taken from their own flesh and blood; and he comes now as their Warrior-Messiah, their Christ. The nations are about to learn a lesson they will never forget about the universal and everlasting kingship of Jesus.

Now the climax comes.

The Lord Yahweh says this: It was of you that I spoke in the past through my servants the prophets of Israel, who prophesied in those days, foretelling your invasion. And it shall come to pass in the Day Gog attacks the land of Israel, declares the Lord Yahweh, that my fury will come up in my face. For in my jealousy and in the fire of my wrath have I spoken:

Surely in that Day there shall be a great shaking in the land of Israel; so that the fishes of the sea and the birds of heaven, and the wild beasts, all the reptiles creeping along the ground, and all people on the face of the earth, will shake at my presence, and the mountains will be thrown down, and cliffs will fall, and every wall will collapse to the ground, and I will summon every kind of sword against him, declares the Lord Yahweh, and each will turn his sword against his comrade. I will punish him with plague and bloodshed, and I will rain down torrential rain, hailstones, fire and brimstone, upon him, upon his troops, and upon the many nations that are with him. I will display my greatness and holiness and I will be known in the eyes of many nations, and they will know that I am the Lord.

- Ezekiel 38:17-23

This is the description of the Great and Terrible Day. His fury will come up in his face. His face will therefore be visible. This is a clear indication in Scripture that Yahweh of Israel will appear visibly on the Great Day, and that the one who will appear on the Great Day is Jesus the Lord, in his humanity. The nations will know that since they marched out against Israel, they have been waging war against Christ the everlasting King.

We can see in this passage that Christ is in complete command of his creation as he weaponizes the forces of nature to defend his people Israel.

'And they will know that I am the Lord,' that I am Jesus, that I am Yahweh of Israel come in the flesh.

These terrifying events will bear fruit in knowledge. The result of Christ's intervention will be the spread, suddenly and dramatically, throughout the world, of the knowledge of the only true God made manifest in his only true Christ. False religion, which is religion hostile to the knowledge of God in Christ, will take itself off in shame at the appearance of the Faithful and True Witness.

Knowledge is the purpose. Knowledge is salvation. Knowledge is healing. When we know who our Savior is, we will call upon him alone, and we will be saved. When we know who our Healer is, we will call upon him alone, and we will be healed. When we seek eternal life, we will know that eternal life is to know the only true God as the Father of Our Lord Jesus Christ.

This, the knowledge of God, will cover the earth as the waters cover the sea, after the world has been woken up by the events of the Great and Terrible Day of the Lord.

So much detail is condensed in this passage that every phrase and every word is worthy of close attention. And this detail is confirmed and clarified in many of the other scriptures we will look at. It may be worth summarizing the things we have picked up from this climactic text before we move to the next passage.

- The events here are centered on Israel, but they affect every part of the earth.
- Yahweh of Israel will become directly involved in the conflict, as he did many times before. This time, he will become present in visible form as the Warrior Christ, and the knowledge gained by the nations will be the knowledge of God in Christ.

- The events that will manifest at his appearing will be so cataclysmic that all the peoples of the earth will be shaking with fear at them.
- One or more nuclear events seem to be indicated. We will see confirmation of this later.
- References to fire and brimstone, when taken together with some other prophetic texts which we will look at, probably refer to oil fields going up in smoke, as in the Fall of Babylon and the cutting down of the harlot of Babylon recounted in Revelation 17 and 18.
- The outcome will be that all the nations on earth will at last know who their true Lord and God is, that he is the God who becomes manifest in Christ, and no other. All the peoples of the earth will be turned away from every form of the occult and idolatry.
- The nations will gain this knowledge from the holiness displayed by Christ when he marches out and saves his people Israel. They will know that Christ is their Savior too when they learn that he is the Savior of his people Israel.

Therefore, son of man, prophesy against Gog, and say, Behold, I am against you Gog, the chief prince of Meshech and Tubal. I will turn you about, lead you, and bring you from the north parts to the mountains of Israel. I will break the bow out of your left hand, and will dash your arrows out of your right hand. You will fall on the mountains of Israel, you, and all your bands, and the nations with you. I will give you as food to ravenous birds of all kinds, and to wild animals.

- Ezekiel 39:1-4

This passage repeats, after several earlier mentions, the information that Yahweh of Israel is against Gog, and that it is he, Yahweh, who will bring Gog and his troops against Israel.

The first reference occurs here to the vultures and jackals and other birds and beasts of prey, which Yahweh will call together in great numbers to gorge themselves on the corpses of the fallen enemies of Israel. It is significant because it links the whole of Ezekiel 38 and 39 to Revelation 19:11-21, the account of the Rider, which also includes a description of the birds of prey being called together to glut themselves on the corpses of the dead.

You will fall in the wilds, for I have spoken, declares the Lord Yahweh. I will send down fire on Magog and on those living undisturbed in the islands, and they will know that I am Yahweh. So I will make my holy Name known by my people Israel, and I will no longer let them profane my holy Name; and the nations will know that I am the Lord, the Holy One in Israel.

- Ezekiel 39:5-7

The holy Name of the Lord has been profaned by his people Israel. This is not the holy Name of Yahweh, which is held in the very highest veneration by the Jewish people. It is the holy Name of Israel's Messiah and ours, the holy Name of Jesus. The Day of the Lord will bring an end to all disrespect for this Name, because it will be known from that Day onward that Jesus is Yahweh of Israel come in the flesh.

And the nations will know that his name is 'holy in Israel.' This is a completely new revelation of the things to come: When God's people Israel come to know that Jesus is their Messiah King, the Gentile nations will know it too. The testimony of Israel to Jesus will be, both to Israel and to the world at large, 'nothing less than life from the dead' (Romans 11:15).

The link drawn so clearly here is at the heart of the message of Ezekiel 38 and 39. The outcome of the Day of the Lord will be the full and unhesitating knowledge of God in Christ among the Jews, the people of Israel, which knowledge will also come to the nations marching against Israel, and to all the nations on earth. What is at stake in the Day of the Lord is the testimony of Israel to Christ, and through them the true knowledge of God in Christ to all the nations on earth.

Behold, it is come, and it is done, says the Lord. This is the Day whereof I have spoken. - Ezekiel 39:8

This is the Day of the Lord, which had been prophesied many times before and would be prophesied many times again. The prophecy is not new. It has been predicted 'in old time by my servants the prophets of Israel' (Ezekiel 38:17).

It is a single event. There is not a multiplicity of Days. There will be the Day of Final Judgment at the close of the age. That is not the Day we are dealing with here. There will be a short conflict before the Day of Judgment, described in Revelation 20:7-10. That is not the conflict we are dealing with here. This long passage of Ezekiel 38 and 39 prophesies the Day of the Lord, a wholly unique event which is also predicted many times elsewhere in Scripture.

And they that dwell in the cities of Israel shall go forth, and shall set on fire and burn the weapons, both the shields and the bucklers, the bows and the arrows, and the javelins, and the spears, and they will burn them for seven years, and they will take no wood from the countryside or cut down any of the forests, for they will be burning the weapons. And they will plunder those who plundered them, and despoil those who despoiled them, says the Lord God.

On that day I will give Gog a famous place in Israel for graves, the valley of the Obarim, east of the sea, the valley that halts the traveler; and there they will bury

Gog and all his multitude, and they will call it the Valley of Hamon-Gog. The house of Israel will take seven months to bury them and cleanse the land. All the people of the land will dig their graves, thus winning themselves renown on the Day when I display my glory, says the Lord Yahweh. And men will be detailed to the permanent duty of going through the land and burying those left above ground and cleansing it. They will begin their search after the seven months, and as they go through the country, if one of them sees any human bones he will set up a marker beside them until the gravediggers have buried them in the Valley of Hamon-Gog (and Hamonah is also the name of a town). Thus shall they cleanse the land. - Ezekiel 39:9-16

This description of the massive and lengthy clean up and burial operation underlines the unimaginable scale of the carnage that will take place on the Day. It is confirmed in the accounts in Revelation, including that of the angel outside Jerusalem, where the blood of the carnage reached up to the horse's bridle as far away as sixteen hundred furlongs from the city (Revelation 14:20).

Son of man, the Lord Yahweh says this, Say to the birds of every kind and to all the wild animals: Muster, come, gather yourselves from every side to my sacrifice I make for you, the great sacrifice on the mountains of Israel, that you may eat flesh and drink blood. You will eat the flesh of the mighty, and drink the blood of the princes of the earth, of rams, of lambs, of goats, and of bullocks, all of them fatlings of Bashan. You will glut yourselves on fat and drink yourselves drunk on blood at this sacrifice I am making for you. You will glut yourselves at my table with horses and chargers, with mighty men and with warriors of all kinds, says the Lord God. - Ezekiel 39:17-20

This elaborated description of the great feast of the birds and wild animals provides detail confirming the link between this description and the description of the Day of the Lord in Revelation 19:11-21. Coming alongside the long period of the burial of the dead, it further emphasizes the scale of the attack against Israel, the vast numbers of the fallen.

And I will display my glory to the nations, and all nations will see my judgment which I have executed, and my hand which I have laid upon them. The House of Israel will know that I am Yahweh their God, from that day forward and forever. - Ezekiel 39:21,22

This latter declaration is absolutely key to understanding the Lord's intentions, the underlying and ultimate purpose of the Day of the Lord. It can only be a prophecy of Israel's coming to faith in Christ. We know that because the text states that Israel will know who he is 'from that day forward and forever.'

The House of Israel had begun to know who Yahweh is from the time of Abraham, who had many and intimate conversations with him. So did the other patriarchs. So did Moses. So did the Judges. So did David and the kings who remained faithful. So did the prophets.

Yet here we have the Lord, speaking through Ezekiel about an event in the far distant future, in 'the end of times,' and saying that in this future time the knowledge of Yahweh is something the house of Israel will acquire for the first time. They will only come to the knowledge of who Yahweh really is on the Day of the Lord, far in the future, in the end times. And the knowledge they will receive on the Great Day will be new knowledge, knowledge they didn't have before.

If the knowledge of Yahweh of Israel which they will receive on the Great Day is only the knowledge of Yahweh of Israel which they already had in Old Testament times, the text would not say that they would know it 'from that day forward and forever.' So what is the new knowledge of Yahweh they will acquire on the Great Day?

There can only be one answer to this. The knowledge they will acquire on the Day of the Lord, which they didn't have before, is the knowledge of God in Christ. Christ will show himself as the true Messiah of Israel on the Great Day.

It will be the fulfillment of the prophecy Jesus spoke outside Jerusalem:

"You will not see my face again until you learn to say, Blessed is he who comes in the name of the Lord."   - Matthew 23:39

The nations too will know that the House of Israel were exiled for their guilt; because they trespassed against me, therefore I hid my face from them, and gave them into the hand of their enemies, so they all fell by the sword. I dealt with them according to their uncleanness and according to their infidelity. - Ezekiel 39:23,24

Again, the link is drawn between the knowledge of God learned by Israel and the knowledge of God learned by the Gentile nations. In both cases it is the knowledge of God in Christ, gained after casting away the abominations of idolatry.

Therefore thus says the Lord God: Now I will bring Jacob's captives back and take pity on the whole House of Israel and show myself jealous for my holy Name. They will forget their disgrace and all the acts of infidelity which they committed against me when they were living safely in their own land, with no one to disturb them. When I bring them home from the peoples, when I gather them back from the countries of their enemies, when I display my holiness in them for

> *many nations to see, they will know that I am Yahweh their God who, having sent them into exile among the nations, have reunited them in their own country, not leaving a single one behind. I will never hide my face from them again, since I will pour out my spirit on the House of Israel, declares the Lord Yahweh.*
>
> *- Ezekiel 39:25-29*

This is the tender language Yahweh uses to let his people know how much he cares for them. He hands them over to their enemies so they will see at last the difference between the horrible gods of the nations, and the God who truly treats them as his own. The expression, 'I will never hide my face from them again,' takes us all the way back to the words of Jesus, 'you will not see my face again <u>until</u> …' These words of Jesus imply that the Day will come when they will indeed see his face again, because on that Day they will learn to say, 'Blessed is he who comes in the Name of the Lord.'

This Day is the Great and Terrible Day of the Lord, frightful for the Lord's enemies, but for those whom he has called, it is the Day on which they will at last be reunited with him in a joy beyond all description. It will be, again in the words of St Paul, 'nothing less than life from the dead.'

As a result of that Day, 'many nations' will realize with a great shock that the God they are called to worship is Yahweh of Israel come in the flesh in Christ. They will never be hostile to Israel again, as they at last know the depth of their debt to Israel.

Just as Israel will wake up with a shock and realize that Jesus really is their Messiah, really is Yahweh of Israel come in the flesh; at the same time, and as a result of the same events, the nations of the earth will also come to realize that the knowledge of God is the knowledge of God made manifest in Christ, or it is not the knowledge of God at all.

There will be no more dabbling in the occult. There will be no more clinging to the sinister spirits hostile to Christ and no more clinging to the religions they hide behind. All, throughout the world, will know that these things are an abomination to the Lord and bring a horrific curse to all who engage in them.

The nations will, because they cling to the true knowledge, the knowledge of God in Christ, enjoy a long period of peace, prophesied in Revelation 20, which will begin long before the end of the world and the Last Judgment.

The knowledge of the only true God is the source of all spiritual power. The floodgates of grace open up to those who know that their God and Savior is Christ the Lord, he alone and there is no other. The floodgates of grace dry up immediately for any member of his kingdom who turns aside to praise other gods.

This is the message we receive at the beginning, the middle, and the end of Scripture. There is only one God, living and true, and he is the one who came among us in Christ. Know this, and you will be blessed. Turn aside from this knowledge and you place yourself under a terrible curse. Speak weasel words about other gods being 'different ways to the same destination,' or 'all the great religions teach the same thing ...'

These deceptions dominate the world of ideas in the age in which I live. They are everywhere, and they are pure spiritual poison. They are the serpentine ideas spread by our spiritual enemies to bring us under spiritual bondage to them and to rob us of our defences against them, to tear us away from the liberating knowledge of Christ and to make us subject to their domination, with all the destructive and horrifying consequences that subjection to sinister spirits brings with it.

It is very difficult for people who grow up with the idea that all religions are good to recognize the essential error in this idea. Once you admit that antichristian religions are good you become incapable of testifying to Christ the King and the only Savior.

The Day of the Lord will clear up the confusion once and for all.

The Day of the Lord will result in the true knowledge of God in Christ covering the earth as the waters cover the sea. The issue is nothing less than whether the peoples of the earth receive the gift and the grace and the peace of God, or whether they continue in horrific subjection to the dark spirits that have nothing to offer us except destruction.

The spiritual warfare has one purpose. The word of God has one purpose. We are led by God to know who he is, to confess his Name, and the Name of his Christ.

> The weapons of our warfare are not carnal but mighty through God to the pulling down of strongholds; casting down imaginations and every high thing that exalts itself against the knowledge of God, and bringing into captivity every thought to the obedience of Christ. — 2 Corinthians 10:4,5

'The knowledge of God.' Knowledge is the purpose. Knowledge is the reason for the word of God. God wants us to know who he is. He wants us to run from the spirits who exalt themselves to rival him. He wants to protect us from the deception of confusing him with his enemies. He wants us to test the spirits, to know which spirits are for him and which spirits are against him. The spirits that confess Christ for who he is, the Son of God come in the flesh, are for him; the spirits that do not confess Christ for who he is are against him (1 John 4:1-4).

This knowledge is our salvation. The presence of Christ is salvation and healing. The presence of Christ is heaven. The presence of his enemies is hell. The knowledge of God in Christ is not only the way to heaven; it *is* heaven.

> "And eternal life is this: to know you, the only true God, and Jesus Christ whom you have sent."
>
> - John 17:3

This is why Ezekiel repeats the phrase so often it is hard to count: 'And then they/you will know that I am the Lord.' The phrase appears at the end of every one of Ezekiel's accounts of the works of the Lord among his people, and among the other peoples of the earth too. Chapters 38 and 39 are no exceptions to this.

> And I will be known in the eyes of many nations, and they will know that I am the Lord.
>
> - Ezekiel 38:23

> And the nations will know that I am the Lord, holy in Israel.   - Ezekiel 39:7

> So the House of Israel will know that I am the Lord their God from that day forward and forever.
>   - Ezekiel 39:22

> When I display my holiness in them for many nations to see, they will know that I am the Lord their God.   - Ezekiel 39:27,28

Ezekiel labors the point because he knows that everything hinges on it. If we know the only true God, the one who saves us in Christ, and place all our trust in him, we will be saved. If we don't know him, if we place our trust in sinister spirits, the spirits who refuse to give their allegiance to him, we will be lost.

It is a simple message. It is the message of Scripture, from beginning to end. Once we understand this, all of Scripture reveals its meaning to us. We have no further need to ask why God gets so angry, why he is so jealous in our regard, why he allows and even arranges such terrible things to befall people. His purpose is to save us.

He sees our need to be saved from the deceptions brought upon us by our enemy the devil and his legions of wicked angels, who dare to rival God for our allegiance even though they have nothing to offer us except destruction; who 'exalt themselves against the knowledge of God.' He does not abandon us to these wicked spirits. He does not leave us in our ignorance. He acts to wake us up before it is too late.

The Great and Terrible Day of the Lord has no other purpose than to bring the peoples of the world, Jews first and then Gentiles, out of their confusion, and into the true knowledge of God in Christ. 'And then,' he says, 'you will know that I am the Lord.'

We have begun with the vivid and detailed account of the Day of the Lord in these two chapters of Ezekiel, 38 and 39. In what follows in this work we will look at the other passages in Scripture which refer to the Day of the Lord. Most of them confirm the details we've just seen Ezekiel 38 and 39. Quite a few of them add to it. None of them contradict it.

There are many descriptions of the Day of the Lord in the Bible and this quality is worth noticing in them. They may highlight different details, but none of them ever contradict any of the others.

ESTHER

At the beginning of the Greek text of the Book of Esther, Mordecai, a devout Jew living at Susa during the time of the Exile, had a dream which he found disturbing.

> This was his dream. There were cries and noise, thunder and earthquakes, and disorder over the whole earth. Then two great dragons came forward, each ready for the fray, and set up a great roar. At the sound of them every nation made ready to wage war against the nation of the just. A day of darkness and gloom, of affliction and distress, oppression and great disturbance on earth! The entire upright nation was thrown into consternation at the fear of the evils awaiting it and prepared for death, crying out to God. Then from its cry, as from a little spring, there grew a great river, a flood of water. Light came as the sun rose, and the humble were raised up and devoured the mighty.   - Esther 1:1d-1k

We can see the pattern repeated here. The two dragons do not feature in Ezekiel's account, but the call to the nations for a military campaign against Israel, the focus on a day, the terror, and the sudden reversal in which the humble of the Lord gain victory over the intimidating hordes coming against them, are all familiar from the account in Ezekiel.

An important feature of this account in Esther is that the 'cries and noise, thunder and earthquakes and disorder' will be spread over the entire earth. It is clear also in later prophecies that the events described by Ezekiel will engage all the peoples of the world. It will be the Great and Terrible Day for all the nations of the earth.

In some of the Old Testament prophecies the 'whole earth' meant the countries of the Middle East and no farther afield. The expression in Esther may be used with this limited reference. However, we will see in other texts that the events described will have worldwide effect.

Later in Esther, the prayer of Mordecai gives us clues about how to prepare for the day of ordeal:

The Day of the Lord Draws Closer

> We have sinned against you
> and you have handed us over to our enemies
> for paying honor to their gods.
>
> — Esther 4:17n

From this diagnosis of the root of the Israelites' troubles, the path to healing can be pointed out.

> Hear my supplication, have mercy on your heritage,
> and turn our grief into rejoicing,
> so that we may live, Lord, to hymn your name.
> Do not suffer the mouths
> of those who praise you to perish.
>
> — Esther 4:17h

The Lord will not allow the mouths of those who praise him to perish. The way to escape the destruction that will take place on the Day of the Lord is to take our place among those whose mouths praise the only true God, the one who came among us in Christ.

THE PSALMS

The Book of the Psalms is peppered with prophetic references to the Day of the Lord. Some of them are condensed into a verse or two. Others are more extended.

> He will rain down red hot coals,
> fire and brimstone on the wicked,
> a horrible tempest will be their portion.
> — Psalm 11:6

This short verse uses the language we find in the other prophecies of the Day of the Lord.

A much more complete picture is provided in the following passage:

> The earth quaked and rocked,
> the mountain's foundations shuddered,
> they quaked at his blazing anger.
> Smoke rose from his nostrils,
> from his mouth devouring fire;

coals were kindled at it.

He parted the heavens and came down,

a storm cloud was under his feet;

he rode on a cherub and flew,

soaring on the wings of the wind.

He made darkness his covering,

his pavilion dark waters and dense cloud.

At the brightness before him the thick clouds passed,

hailstones and coals of fire.

The Lord thundered in the heavens,

the Most High made his voice heard.

He shot his arrows and scattered them,

he shot out lightnings and routed them.

The very springs of the ocean were exposed,

the world's foundations were laid bare,

at your rebuke, O Lord,

at the blast of the breath of your nostrils.

     - Psalm 18:7-15

This is easily recognized as a confirmatory account of the description in Ezekiel 38 and 39. It indicates strongly that the Incarnate Lord will make a visible appearance on the Great Day. The point is not certain, the descriptions of a man acting could be symbolic, but the text can be credibly read as a recounting of a vision of an appearance of the Lord in the flesh. Later in this work we will see further and more explicit indications that he will become personally, visibly and decisively engaged in the action when the Day arrives.

A short restatement of the prophecy is contained in these verses:

> You will make them as a fiery oven
> on the day of your anger ...
> For they intended evil against you,
> but plot as they may, they will not succeed,
> since you will make them turn tail
> by shooting your arrows in their faces.
> - Psalm 21:9-12

Here too, there is a strong indication that Our Lord himself will become engaged in the conflict, by 'shooting his arrows in their faces.'

Psalm 46 recounts some of the events of the Great Day and includes theological reassurance as well.

> God is for us a refuge and strength …
> so we will not fear though the earth should rock,
> though mountains tumble into the midst of the sea,
> and its waters roar and seethe …
> God is in the city, it cannot fall;
> at break of day God comes to its rescue.
> Nations are in uproar,
> kingdoms are tumbling,
> when he raises his voice
> the earth crumbles away …
> He breaks the bow, he snaps the spear,
> the shields he burns in the fire.
> Be still and know that I am God,
> supreme over nations, supreme on the earth.
> — Psalm 46:1-10

This deeply calming psalm tells us that even in the midst of the disturbances of the Day of the Lord, we can be at peace, assured that God is in total control and that the outcome will be the establishment of his kingdom in every nation on earth. The details of the earth rocking, mountains tumbling into the sea, the waters roaring and seething, are in stark contrast with the holy city (Jerusalem and the church) which cannot be shaken because God himself dwells within it.

> For look, the kings made alliance,
> together they advanced;
> they saw, and they panicked;
> they were troubled,
> and they fled away.
> Trembling seized them there,
> and pain, as of a woman in travail.
> By the east wind you have destroyed
> the ships of Tarshish.
>
> - Psalm 48:4-7

The detail in the last verse tells us that the conflict on the Day of the Lord will not only be on land. Tarshish was a city on the southern coast of Turkey. Ezekiel 38 and 39 describe a massive military engagement on land only. Here in Psalm 48, we have a brief reference to a naval defeat.

There has already been one fulfillment of this prophecy. There will probably be a further fulfillment when the Day of the Lord arrives. The fulfillment which has already taken place was at the Battle of Lepanto in 1571 A.D., in which the Ottoman navy, the most powerful military fleet in the world at the time, sailing toward western Europe with the intention of imposing Islam there, was met by a mixed fleet of Spanish and other European vessels, called together at the request of Pope Pius V and supported by the praying of the rosary across southern Europe.

Against the run of play, so to speak, a sudden, wholly unexpected east wind threw the Ottoman fleet into disarray and all its ships were destroyed. The decisive victory at Lepanto secured the churches in Europe for the following four centuries; and not only the churches in Europe, but all their offshoots in other parts of the world as well.

In Psalm 68 we find references to the Day of the Lord scattered through the text.

> Let God arise, let his foes be scattered,
> let those who hate him flee before him.
> You disperse them like smoke;
> as wax melts in the presence of a fire,
> so the wicked melt at the presence of God.
> - Psalm 68:1,2

Verses 4 and 33 of Psalm 68 refer to the Lord as 'the Rider of the clouds,' and 'the Rider of the Heavens,' prefiguring Revelation 19:11,19,21, in which the Lord comes forth at the head of the armies of heaven as the victorious 'Rider.'

> God, when you set out at the head of your people,
> when you strode over the desert, the earth rocked,
> the heavens pelted down rain at the presence of God,
> at the presence of God, the God of Israel.
> - Psalm 68:7,8

This passage is significant for two things. It confirms the expectation that the Lord will take charge of the warfare personally on the Great Day; and it indicates that he will come from 'the desert.' The desert, in the mind of an Israelite, is Arabia. We will see other texts in which this prediction is also made, that when Christ appears on the Great Day, he will be coming from the desert of Arabia.

> They perish at the rebuke of your countenance.
> - Psalm 80:16

This is a one line reference to the central event in the Day of the Lord, when the Lord's fury will suddenly come up in his face (Ezekiel 38:18) and his enemies, seized with sudden terror, will be thrown into helpless confusion at the sight.

> Cloud and darkness are round about him,
> righteousness and justice the foundations of his
>   throne.
> Fire goes before him
> and burns up his enemies round about;
> his lightning flashes light up the world,

> the earth sees it and trembles.
>
> The mountains melt like wax
>
> before the Lord of all the earth.
>
> The heavens declare his righteousness
>
> and all nations see his glory.
>
> Shame on all who serve images,
>
> who pride themselves on their idols;
>
> worship him, all you spirits.
>
> - Psalm 97:2-7

The result of these events is particularly clear in this text. All the nations will see his glory, when he acts on behalf of his people. Seeing his glory, they will immediately be ashamed of their idolatry and will worship only him, the true God, the one who manifests himself in Christ.

Psalm 110 adds further light on this. The Lord will be established as king of all the earth only after victory in a terrible conflict.

> The Lord who sits at your right hand
>
> will shatter kings in the day of his wrath.

> He will judge the nations, heaping up corpses,
> he will break heads over the whole wide world.
>
> - Psalm 110:5,6

A further text, in Psalm 144, describes the Lord as coming down from the heavens and entering into the conflict.

> Part the heavens O Lord, and come down,
> touch the mountains and make them smoke.
> Scatter them with continuous lightning flashes,
> rout them with a volley of your arrows.
>
> - Psalm 144:5,6

'Mountains' here symbolize peoples and their rulers, the powerful nations of the earth who come against Israel, God's chosen people.

The evidence from the Psalms is very strong, almost conclusive, that the Lord will make a visible appearance, in his humanity, on the Great and Terrible Day. 'Continuous lightning flashes' will be the garment, so to speak, worn by Christ when he appears on the Day. This is clear also in numerous other texts, such as Isaiah 2:10,19,21 (repeated three times for emphasis), Habakkuk 3:11, Matthew 24:27, Luke 17:24, Revelation 16:18.

The Psalms are consistent too with Ezekiel 38 and 39 in mentioning hailstones, mountains crumbling, the seas in turmoil, and vast numbers of dead.

WISDOM

The Book of Wisdom gives us some unique insights into the causes and the results of the Day of the Lord.

> For armor he will take his jealous love,
> he will arm creation to punish his enemies.
> — Wisdom 5:17

Two distinct truths are condensed in this verse. First, the 'jealous love' of God is what informs all his dealings with his people. The spiritual warfare in the high places is a contest for our allegiance. For us everything, absolutely everything, depends on whether we place our trust in the true God and in his Christ, or whether we turn away and join the rebel spirits to serve the horrible prince of darkness. Satan always seeks to rival God for our allegiance. And he has a particularly intense hatred for the knowledge we gain from the doctrine of the Incarnation.

God's love is therefore 'jealous' in our regard. 'He jealously desires the spirit that he has made to dwell within us' (James 4:5). He wants us to stay with him and not to go over to his spiritual rivals. He wants us to have nothing to do with other gods, nothing to do with the sinister spirits and the religions, the fashions, the deceptions, the occult practices they hide behind.

His 'jealous love,' sometimes called 'zeal,' is what drives God to fight on our behalf. When he comes to lead the troops on the Great and Terrible Day, his motivation will be his 'jealous love' for us, his desire to win back our allegiance from his enemies and ours.

The second truth in Wisdom 5:17 is that God will turn his Creation into so many armaments to inflict terror and defeat on his enemies, the enemies who come against his people. Watch how the list of God's own strengths runs into the list of the created things he uses as weapons.

> He will put on justice as a breastplate,
> and for helmet wear his forthright judgment;
> he will take up invincible holiness for shield,
> of his pitiless wrath he will forge a sword.
>
>   - Wisdom 5:18-20

Thus far the imagery presages the imagery used by St Paul in Ephesians 6:14-17, detailing the armor, defensive and offensive, of the soldier in the spiritual warfare.

The description follows immediately of the weaponizing of God's creatures for use against his enemies. It is a recounting of the destruction described in the other prophecies of the Day of the Lord.

> And the universe will march with him
> to fight the reckless.
> Bolts truly aimed, the shafts of lightning will leap,
> and from the clouds, as from a full drawn bow,
> fly to their mark;
> and the catapult will hurl hailstones charged with
> > fury.
> The waters of the sea will rage against them,
> the rivers engulf them without pity,
> a mighty gale will rise against them
> and winnow them like a hurricane.
> > - Wisdom 5:20-23

The passage concludes with something I haven't seen in any of the other prophecies. It places the entire responsibility for the catastrophe on the evildoers themselves. It does not place the responsibility on God, as other texts seem to do. It places the responsibility on the wicked.

> Thus wickedness will lay the whole earth waste,
> and evildoing bring down the thrones of the mighty.
>   - Wisdom 5:23

The author of the Book of Wisdom clearly felt the need to wrestle with this question: how can the good God involve himself actively and visibly in our war? The question is frequently answered with an assertion that God permits evil, he permits sin and the consequences of sin, but God himself never does evil to anyone. He watches sadly as humans step onto Satan's ground and suffer the consequences of belonging to Satan's horrible kingdom, but God himself inflicts no harm on anyone, not even on the wicked.

It's a thorny question. I've always been drawn to the view that God only knows how to rescue us from harm. He never inflicts harm himself. And yet, if war is sometimes necessary and just, and if soldiers are commended for fighting to the death in a just war, is there any good reason why Christ should be prohibited from doing the same? When he sees his people under attack from an enemy bent on their destruction, are we to be squeamish about the idea that he will, at a moment chosen by himself, enter decisively into the battle to defend his people against the enemies determined to destroy them?

The Book of Wisdom, in the passages quoted above, makes it clear that he will indeed make a decisive intervention in the warfare, and he will do so without incurring the slightest blame. The blame will fall entirely on the wicked, and the cause of the destruction will be their evildoing.

The result of the warfare is then spelt out. The result will be regime change in all the nations of the earth. Evildoing will 'bring down the thrones of the mighty.' The thrones of the rulers of the earth will be brought down, and the thrones of the sinister spirits in the hearts and souls of men will be brought down. Christ will be accepted as king, by nations and by individuals.

Chapter 6 goes on to issue a warning to rulers of the earth in terms strongly reminiscent of Psalm 2:10-12.

> Listen then, kings and understand ...
> for sovereignty is given to you by the Lord,
> and power by the Most High ...
> if therefore you have not ruled justly,
> as servants of his kingdom, nor observed the law,
> nor followed the will of God,
> he will fall on you swiftly and terribly.
> On the highly placed a ruthless judgment falls.
> - Wisdom 6:1-5

The truths about the Great Day set out in this Book are of the highest importance, and some of them are not found elsewhere in the prophecies. It may therefore be worth listing them here.

- The warfare on the Day of the Lord is spiritual warfare. It happens because of the contest for our allegiance between spiritual powers, the power of God and his Christ on one hand, and that of Satan and his wicked angels on the other.
- Christ, as well as exercising his own spiritual authority in the warfare, and as well as becoming visibly engaged at the head of the combat, will also, on the Great Day, weaponize his creation against the enemies of his people, so that 'the universe will march with him.'
- The responsibility for the carnage and destruction will not belong to Christ; it will belong to the wicked and their evil doings.
- The result of the warfare will be regime change in the nations and individuals of the world. The rule of the wicked will be brought down.
- All the rulers of the earth receive their power from God. If they do not honor him and keep his laws, their way will come to swift destruction.

ISAIAH

A number of passages in Isaiah contain key information about the Great Day. The first of these is Isaiah 2:10-21.

> Go into the rock, hide in the dust,
> in terror of Yahweh,
> at the brilliance of his majesty,
> when he arises to make the earth quake.
>   - Isaiah 2:10, repeated in 2:19 and 2:21

Isaiah visualizes what is to happen in the future with great clarity and power. In this verse he describes the Lord arising 'to make the earth quake,' causing terror among the people 'at the brilliance of his majesty.' These terms make it very difficult to deny that on the Day of the Lord he will appear in visible form, in his humanity, and his presence will be plain for all to see.

The scene described here is similar to that described in Revelation 6:12-17, in which all the kings of the earth 'hid in caverns and among the rocks of the mountains. They said to the mountains and the rocks, "Fall on us and hide us away from the One who sits on the throne and from the retribution of the Lamb. For the Great Day of his retribution has come, and who can stand before it?'" (Revelation 6:15-17).

> Human pride will lower its eyes,
> human arrogance will be humbled,
> and Yahweh alone will be exalted on that day.
> - Isaiah 2:11, repeated in 2:17

The only true Lord, and he alone, will be exalted on that Day. In the Bible, when God's people get themselves into serious trouble, idolatry in one form or another is at the root of it.

> That day, men will fling to moles and bats their idols of silver and their idols of gold which have been made for them to worship.   - Isaiah 2:20

Brief descriptions of the Day of the Lord are contained in Isaiah 5:25-30, Isaiah 13:4-14, and Isaiah 17:12-14.

An extended treatment is given in Isaiah 24:17-23, which ends with an affirmation that it is in Jerusalem that the Lord will be glorified on the Great Day.

The central place of Jerusalem (referred to here as Ariel) in the events is highlighted also in Isaiah 29:1-8.

> Woe to Ariel, Ariel, the city where David encamped
> ...
> the horde of your enemies will be like fine dust,
> the horde of the warriors like flying chaff.
> And suddenly, in an instant,
> you will be visited by Yahweh Sabaoth,
> with thunder, earthquake, mighty din,
> hurricane and tempest,
> and the flame of devouring fire.
> It will be like a dream, like a vision at night,
> the horde of all the nations at war with Ariel,
> all those fighting, besieging and troubling it.
> It will be as when a hungry man dreams,
> and eats, then awakes with a hungry belly;
> or when a thirsty man dreams he drinks,
> then wakes up exhausted and with a parched throat.

> So will it be with the hordes of all the nations
> making war on Mount Zion.
>
>   - Isaiah 29:1-8

The suddenness of the turnaround in fortunes, when the Lord visits Mount Zion at the climax of the warfare, is very vividly described here. The vast horde of the enemies of Jerusalem will suddenly find themselves like those who wake up from a dream in which they were certain of the satisfaction of their desires, only to find their hopes dashed.

Isaiah 34:1-10 contains one of several references to the place of Arabia in the Great Day. The passage begins with the theme of Yahweh's anger with the nations of the earth.

> Let the earth hear, and all that is therein,
> the world, and all its population,
> for the indignation of the Lord is upon all the nations,
> and his fury is upon all their armies.
> He has vowed them to destruction,
> handed them over to slaughter.

The Day of the Lord Draws Closer

> Their slain shall be cast out,
> and their stink shall come up out of their carcasses,
> the mountains shall run with their blood,
> and all the host of heaven shall be dissolved,
> and all their host will fall down.
>
>   - Isaiah 34:1-4

The repulsive detail here about the stink of the dead 'coming up out of their carcasses' can perhaps help us understand why the Lord calls on the birds of prey and the wild animals to gather together and glut themselves on the remains of the fallen. There will be such a great mass of the dead in Israel that it will take a long time to bury them, and it will thus become urgently necessary to dispose of their remains.

The text then turns to Edom (Arabia).

> For my sword has drunk deep in the heavens:
> see how it now falls on Edom …
> For Yahweh has a sacrifice in Bozrah,
> A great slaughter in the land of Edom …
> their land will be drenched in blood,

and their dust will be greasy with fat.

For it is the Day of the Lord's vengeance,

and the year of retribution for the controversy of Zion.

- Isaiah 34:5-8

'The controversy of Zion.' How familiar that expression is in our own day, more than two and a half thousand years after Isaiah wrote this text. There is a controversy about Zion. It has been a cup of provocation in the world ever since King David settled the ark of the covenant in Jerusalem about three thousand years ago. It is the most long standing controversy in history, just as anti Semitism is the most long standing hostility in history.

'The controversy of Zion' is so long standing because its roots are spiritual. It is at the heart of the warfare between God and the creature who seeks to raise himself aloft to rival God.

Satan, our ancient enemy, has set himself implacably against the Jews for one simple reason, spoken by Christ:

'Salvation is of the Jews.'   - John 4:22

The whole purpose of the existence of the Jews as a separate people is that they are called by God to be his people. They are the people to whom God chose to entrust himself as Flesh of their flesh and Blood of their blood. Christ, the greatest Jew, is the purpose of their existence as a separate people. That is why the spirit of Antichrist is not friendly toward the Jews. He never was, and never will be.

'The controversy of Zion' has not yet been resolved. It will be resolved on the Day of the Lord. Right up to the present time there have been wars and threats of war over the question of who owns Jerusalem, and who has stewardship of it. The reason for this is that 'the controversy of Zion' is rooted in the ancient conflict between Christ and Antichrist. Christ came into the world as a member of a people. That people is the Jews. He was a Jew when he was born, and he remains a Jew forever. That is why the spirit of Antichrist is at war with the Jews. It is part of his warfare against Christ and Christ's followers.

See what will happen in Arabia on that Day:

> Its streams will be turned into pitch,
> and its dust into brimstone
> its country will be turned into blazing pitch.
> It will not be quenched day or night,
> its smoke will go up forever.
>
> - Isaiah 34:9,10

This refers to the 'fire and brimstone' rained down on the nations attacking Israel as prophesied in Ezekiel 38:22, and the fall of Babylon prophesied in several scriptures and elaborated in Revelation 17 and 18.

The harlot of Babylon and her fall have very deep spiritual significance. We will return to this in discussing Revelation 17 and 18.

Isaiah 63 describes the Lord himself becoming involved in the bloody conflict when the Great and Terrible Day comes. It shows him taking sole charge of the warfare, with no one coming to his help, at least for a time. These verses are not for the hypersensitive.

The Day of the Lord Draws Closer

Who is this coming up from Edom,

from Bozrah with crimson garments,

so glorious in his apparel, marching in great strength?

It is I that speak in righteousness, mighty to save.

Why are your garments red,

your clothes like someone treading the winepress?

I have trodden the winepress alone;

of my people not one was with me.

So I trod them down in my anger,

I trampled them in my wrath.

Their blood sprinkled over my garments,

and all my clothes are stained.

For I have decided on a Day of vengeance,

my year of retribution has come.

I looked, there was no one to help me,

and I wondered that I could find no supporter.

Then my own arm came to my rescue,

and my own fury upheld me.

I crushed the peoples in my anger,

I shattered them in my fury,

and sent their blood streaming to the ground.

- Isaiah 63:1-6

Much detail is missing, but this much, affirmed in other texts also, is clear in this passage.

- The Lord will make a visible appearance on the Great Day, in his humanity.
- He will act as a warrior, mighty in battle.
- He will act on his own authority, not relying on anyone else.
- He will come 'from Edom,' from Arabia.
- His fury will be against the nations who attack his people Israel; his garments were already red when he arrived from Bozrah.

Isaiah 5:12-14, 24:5,6, and Chapters 42-48 - these texts are not directly concerned with the Day of the Lord, but they reveal much about God's motivation in taking action on the great and terrible Day. The problem is not only with the enemies of God's people. God's people are a problem to themselves. They need to be rescued from themselves.

> Never a thought for the works of the Lord,
>
> never a glance at what his hands have done.
>
> That is why my people are in captivity,
>
> because they have no knowledge;
>
> their dignitaries are famished,
>
> their populace parched with thirst.
>
> That is why hell opens wide its jaws,
>
> and gapes with measureless throat,
>
> and down go her noblemen and people.
>
> - Isaiah 5:12-14

'Because they have no knowledge.' The knowledge of God in Christ is alien to them. That is why they have brought so much trouble on themselves. God expects us to notice the things he does for us, and he expects us to give the glory where it belongs, to him alone.

Praise is of the highest importance, not because God needs to receive it, but because we need to give it. We are called to 'offer to God the continual sacrifice of praise, the fruit of the lips of those who confess his name' (Hebrews 13:15). Praise is a sacrifice, and we are not to sacrifice to other gods. When we praise them we are sacrificing to them; and sacrificing to other gods places us under the biblical curse of destruction (Exodus 22:19).

> The earth is defiled by the feet of its inhabitants
> because they have transgressed the laws,
> changed the ordinance, broken the everlasting covenant.
> That is why the curse has devoured the earth,
> and those who dwell in it are desolate;
> that is why the inhabitants of the earth
> are burnt up, and few men are left.
> — Isaiah 24:5,6

They have 'changed the ordinance.' There is very precise information here as to the root reasons for the trouble we are building up for ourselves. The perversion of morals I have seen in my lifetime is unprecedented in history, both in its scope and in the speed with which it has happened. People have always done immoral things, but in the age I live in they have mobilized every institution in civic life to establish and enforce the falsehood that evil deeds are good. The most abominable practices have been legalized, promoted through all media, recommended to schoolchildren from their earliest years, and laws are passed forbidding anyone to do or say anything to oppose them.

God is not standing idly by as these assaults are made against his honor and the dignity of his children. For this reason the Day of the Lord might not be as far in the future as we might wish to think.

'I am the Lord, and there is no other.' 'I will not yield my glory to another, nor my honor to idols.' These and similar expressions are repeated throughout chapters 42-48 of Isaiah. The root of the root is being exposed here. Purity of faith, purity of worship, this is what keeps us covered by the blessing of God and powerfully protected from our enemies. Spiritual fornication, turning aside to other gods, praising the spirits that reject Christ and the occult practices and religions they hide behind, mixing the true worship with the false, these are the things God most hates, the root causes of all other sins and the root reason people get themselves into a mess.

When the Day of the Lord comes, it will be to clean up all these things, to set us free from them so that they will not appear among us again.

> Things now past I revealed long ago,
> they issued from my mouth, I proclaimed them;
> suddenly I acted and they came to pass;
> because I knew you are obstinate,
> your neck an iron sinew and your forehead bronze.
> I declared it to you from the beginning,
> before it came to pass I revealed it to you,
> so that you could not say, 'my idol has done it,
> my graven image, my metal idol has commanded it.'
> - Isaiah 48:3-5

This is a key passage for understanding the purpose of prophecy. God tells us again and again that he does not want us to give his glory to another, he does not want us to give his honor to idols. He uses the prophets to predict future events so that when they occur we will recall that it was he, our God and Savior, who ordained and foretold them. 'And then,' as he tells us so frequently through the prophet Ezekiel, 'you will know that I am the Lord.'

JEREMIAH

The Book of Jeremiah contains some of the earliest and clearest indications that the Day of the Lord will affect not only Israel and Jerusalem, but the entire world. He shows how earnest he is about making this point by repeating it frequently and in arresting language. The Lord is about to bring disaster on the city which is the apple of his eye, Jerusalem, so how can the other nations of the earth imagine they will be spared?

Jeremiah 25:15-33

Yahweh hands Jeremiah a cup of the wine of his wrath, telling him to make all the nations of the earth drink it. Those nations are listed.

> "They will drink, and reel and lose their wits, because of the sword I am sending among them." I took the cup from Yahweh's hand and made all the nations to whom Yahweh sent me drink it: Jerusalem and the towns of Judah ... Pharaoh king of Egypt ... all the kings of the country of the

> Philistines ... Edom, Moab, the king of Tyre, the kings of Sidon ... Dedan ... all the kings of Arabia ... all the kings of Elam, and all the kings of Media; all the kings of the north, near and far, one after another; in short, all the kingdoms on the face of the earth; and the king of Sheshak will drink last of all.
>
> - Jeremiah 25:18-26

The wrath of the Lord is directed first against Jerusalem, and then against every nation on the face of the earth.

> If they refuse to take the cup from your hand and drink, you will say to them, 'Yahweh Sabaoth says this: you must drink! Look, I am beginning to bring disaster on the city which is called by my name, so are you likely to go unpunished?'
>
> - Jeremiah 25:27-29

The carnage that will take place on that Day will spread to every part of the world.

> Yahweh Sabaoth says this: Look, disaster is spreading from nation to nation, a mighty tempest is rising from the far ends of the earth. The slain of the Lord on that day will be scattered across the world from end to end. They will not be lamented; no one will gather them or bury them; they will lie on the ground like dung. - Jeremiah 25:32,33

Jeremiah 46:9,10

This brief account of the Day of the Lord lists some of the countries that will come against Israel, confirming in part the list in Ezekiel 38:2-6.

> Charge, horses! Forward chariots!
> Let the warriors advance,
> men from Cush and Put with shield in hand,
> men from Lud who bend the bow!
> For this is the Day of Lord Yahweh Sabaoth,
> a day of vengeance
> when he takes revenge on his foes.
> - Jeremiah 46:9,10

The countries listed here are Sudan/Somalia (Cush), Libya (Put) and Lydia (Lud) which is part of modern Turkey.

Jeremiah 51:1-19

This passage is ostensibly about the fall of Babylon after the Exile. It is a good example of the multilayered significances we find in biblical prophecy, because its reference moves from the fall of Babylon two and a half thousand years ago, to the fall of the great harlot of Babylon at the time of the Day of the Lord, prophesied in much greater detail in Revelation 17 and 18.

> Flee out of the midst of Babylon,
> and deliver every man his own soul;
> do not perish for her iniquity,
> for now is the time for Yahweh's vengeance.
> - Jeremiah 51:6

This verse begins to indicate that the fall of Babylon after the Exile prefigures the later events, in the end time in which the Day of the Lord will occur. The following verse anticipates what the Book of Revelation says about that time.

> Babylon was a golden cup
> in Yahweh's hand
> that has made all the earth drunk;
> the nations drank her wine
> and then went mad.
> - Jeremiah 51:7

This clearly prefigures Revelation 17:2-4 about the harlot of Babylon 'who has made all the inhabitants of the earth drunk with the wine of her fornication' and who 'had a golden cup in her hand full of the abominations and filthiness of her fornication.' We are undoubtedly looking at end times prophecy here, whose significance was not exhausted in the fall of Babylon at the end of the Exile in the late 500s b.c.

> Enthroned beside abundant waters,
> rich in treasures, you now meet your end.
> - Jeremiah 51:13

Recall that the harlot of Babylon in Revelation 17:1 is 'enthroned beside abundant waters.'

What follows is a brief description of the Day of the Lord.

> When he thunders,
> there is a roaring of waters in heaven;
> he raises clouds
> from the farthest ends of the earth;
> he makes the lightning flash for the downpour,
> and brings the wind from his storehouse.
>
> — Jeremiah 51:16

Jeremiah then turns, as he often does, to the root cause of the trouble, which is the worship of other gods.

> At this everyone stands stupefied, uncomprehending;
> every goldsmith blushes for his idols;
> his castings are but a delusion, with no breath in them.
> They are futile, a laughable production;
> when the time of their visitation comes,

they will perish.

The Heritage of Jacob is not like these,

for he is the maker of everything

and Israel is the rod of his inheritance;

Yahweh Sabaoth is his name.

- Jeremiah 51:17-19

The significance of the harlot of Babylon is very deep. It has to do with idolatry affecting all the rulers and all the peoples of the earth, spiritual fornication which always results also in fornication in the flesh.

The spiritual and carnal fornication are the root cause, the reason the Day of the Lord is necessary. And the Day of the Lord is the remedy for spiritual and carnal fornication. When he appears and acts on that Day, it will no longer be possible to maintain the delusion that other gods can replace him.

OTHER TEXTS IN EZEKIEL

Apart from the description in Chapters 38 and 39, Ezekiel has a number of other confirmatory references to the Day of the Lord.

Ezekiel 30:1-5

This brief description of the Day of the Lord lists some of the countries which will join the expedition. It adds both Egypt and Arabia to the list in Ezekiel 38:2-6.

> Howl: Disaster day! For the day is near, the day of the Lord is near. It will be a day dark with cloud, a time of doom for the nations. The sword will come on Egypt, and anguish on the land of Cush when the slaughtered fall in Egypt, when her riches are carried away and her foundations are destroyed. Cush, Put and Lydia, all Arabia, Chub and the country of the covenant will fall by the sword with them.
>
> - Ezekiel 30:2-5

Chub is within the boundaries of modern Libya. Ezekiel goes on, as always, to say what the end result will be. 'And they will know that I am the Lord' – repeated four times in the chapter (30:8,19,25,26). They will know that Yahweh of Israel who came in the flesh in Christ is the true Lord and God, the true Savior, the one who makes a terrifying appearance on the Day of the Lord.

Ezekiel 32:17-32

This lament for Egypt and all the 'famous nations' which will go down with her on the Day of the Lord, confirms Ezekiel's other lists of nations and adds Assyria and 'the Sidonians.'

> "Son of man, wail over the multitude of Egypt, for down she must go with the daughters of famous nations to the depths of the nether world with those who go down into the pit ... Assyria is there, and all her hordes ... all of them slaughtered, fallen by the sword ... Elam *(Iran)* is there and all her throng ... Meshech and Tubal *(Turkey)* are there and all her

throng ... Edom *(Arabia)* is there ... All the princes of the north and all the Sidonians are there, who have gone down with the slaughtered."

- Ezekiel 32:18-30

DANIEL

The prophecies in the Book of Daniel have an extraordinary power to command our attention. The book is set in the time of the Exile and was written during the Exile or shortly afterwards.

The end time prophecies in Daniel speak of warfare in the heavenly places. The warfare takes effect in the broader world rather than being restricted to Jerusalem and Israel. Of all the Old Testament prophecies they have most in common with the end times prophecies in the New Testament, those spoken by Jesus, by Paul to the Thessalonians, and in the Book of Revelation.

Like so many of the other prophecies, the prophecies in Daniel have multiple layers of fulfillment. They were fulfilled in part a few centuries later in the time of the Maccabees. They were fulfilled again in part when the Temple in Jerusalem was destroyed in 70 a.d. And they will see further fulfillment in the years leading up to the Day of the Lord.

At the end of the prophecies of turmoil in Chapter 7, when evil persons, 'beasts,' have been ruling over the empires of the world, Daniel speaks of the Messiah King:

> I was gazing into the visions of the night,
> when I saw, coming on the clouds of heaven,
> one like a Son of Man.
> He came to the Ancient of Days,
> and was brought near before him.
> To him was given dominion, and glory, and kingship,
> and all peoples and nations and languages
> became his servants.
> His rule is an everlasting rule
> that will never pass away,
> and his kingship will never come to an end.
>
> *- Daniel 7:13,14*

The meaning of this passage includes but is not restricted to the Second Coming of Our Lord at the close of the age. This point is very important. Jesus started coming on the clouds of heaven at the time of his sacrificial Death and Resurrection. "From this time onward," Jesus said, immediately before his conviction and sentencing, "you will see the Son of Man seated at the right hand of the Power and coming on the clouds of heaven" (Matthew 26:64).

His kingship over all the nations has already begun; it will be clearly manifest to all nations from the time of the Day of the Lord; and it will be complete from the Day of Judgment.

Daniel goes on to describe the period immediately preceding the Day of the Lord, the depths of slavery to Satan into which the world will fall and which will necessitate the Lord's intervention. The man of iniquity, prophesied later as coming immediately before the Day of the Lord (2 Thessalonians 2:2-4) is described in Daniel 7:25,26.

> He will insult the Most High, and torment the holy ones of the Most High. He will plan to alter the seasons and the laws, and the saints will be handed over to him for a time, two times and half a time.
>
> - Daniel 7:25

This period of three and a half years is mentioned in other parts of Scripture. It is the duration in which Satan will appear to be in total control of all the peoples of the earth. The famine in the time of Elijah lasted this long. See also Revelation 12:14, the time during which the woman, the Mother of the Son who is the target of the dragon's hatred, will be protected from the distress.

The activities of the 'horn,' which in biblical prophecy means a ruler and his empire, symbolized by the power of a horn to amplify messages, i.e., to take control of the means of communication and hence of the spread of information and propaganda, are further described:

> ... a horn which grew to great size toward south and east and toward the Land of Splendor. It grew right up to the armies of heaven and flung armies and stars to the ground, and trampled them underfoot. It even challenged the power of the Prince of the army. It abolished the perpetual sacrifice and overthrew the foundation of his sanctuary, and the army too. Over

the sacrifice it installed iniquity and flung truth to the ground. The horn was active and successful.
- Daniel 8:9-12

The abolition of the daily sacrifice (the Mass) and the installation of the abomination of desolation (a perverted ritual presented as if it were the real Eucharist) in its place is prophesied three times in Daniel, and repeated by Jesus in his prophetic words in the gospels. These repetitions underline the central place of these events in the prophecies.

He will strike a firm alliance with many people for the space of one week; and in the middle of one week he will cause the sacrifice and oblation to cease, and on the wing of the Temple will be the abomination of desolation until the end, until the doom assigned to the devastator.   - Daniel 9:27

He will abolish the perpetual sacrifice and install the abomination of desolation there. Those who break the covenant he will seduce by his blandishments,

> but the people who know their God will stand firm and take action. ... He will grow more and more arrogant, considering himself greater than all the gods; he will utter incredible blasphemies against the God of gods, and he will thrive until the wrath reaches bursting point; for what has been decreed will certainly be fulfilled. Neither shall he regard the God of his fathers, nor the desire of women, nor regard any god, for he shall magnify himself above all. Instead, he will honor the god of fortresses.
>
> - Daniel 11:31-38

This is a detailed profile of the Antichrist. It could be a profile of the kind of person who would lead a great army, with a host of the armies of many other nations, against Israel in an attempt to take ownership of Jerusalem, though this is uncertain because we do not know if the Antichrist is identified with the Gog of Ezekiel 38 and 39. In spite of his success, he will soon fall to 'the doom assigned to the devastator' (Daniel 9:27).

Who is the Antichrist? Is it a spirit? Is it a man? Is it a collection of spirits or a collection of men?

It is all these. In 2 Thessalonians Paul speaks of the Wicked One, the Lost One, 'the Enemy who raises himself above every so called god or object of worship to enthrone himself in God's sanctuary and flaunts the claim that he is God' (2 Thessalonians 2:3,4). This, of course, is Satan. And it is also the spirit of Satan who will work through a particular man immediately before the Day of the Lord, probably by diabolical possession, and who is already at work in other wicked spirits and in humans. This is why the apostle John tells us that 'the Antichrist is coming' and in the same verse he tells us that 'many Antichrists have already come' (1 John 2:18).

Most of the detail in these texts in Daniel indicate that the man of iniquity, who is the Antichrist, will be a secular leader who exalts himself to great heights, even appointing himself to take fake authority over the church. Because he will be acting as a man, it seems likely that he will be doing so by some form of diabolical possession.

The man of iniquity will have these qualities:

- He will subjugate many nations
- He will be arrogant beyond measure
- He will scorn and blaspheme God
- He will propose himself as a superior god
- He will be skilful in doing deals and will seduce many peoples
- He will rely on brute power as his god
- He will exalt homosexuality
- He will gain spurious control over the church.
- He will abolish the daily sacrifice (the Holy Sacrifice of the Mass)
- He will replace the Mass with the abomination of desolation, probably a hoax eucharist of some kind, concocted from a syncretism of various religious and occult practices.
- He will come to a swift end on the Day the Lord intervenes to save his people.

There is a great wealth of information here concerning the period immediately preceding the Day of the Lord.

This information is consistent with the information we have in the New Testament. It helps us to read the signs of the times.

Will these things happen in our lifetimes, as I write this? We don't know the timescale. God has not revealed the times and seasons to us.

I don't take the view that we are anywhere close to the events described in these texts in Daniel. My view is that they will take place in a future century, not in this one. But one can see some of the trends building up. The explosion in apostasy, in people turning to occult practice and religion, the public approval given to homosexual practice in western countries, all of this gives serious cause for alarm. In all honesty, when we see these things happening it is right to take warning from them.

JOEL

Joel makes it clear, early in his account, that the Day of the Lord will be preceded by the loss of 'the grain offering and the drink offering' (Joel 1:9). This prophecy has reference to the Temple worship in Jerusalem, but it also has reference to the dereliction that will come upon the church immediately preceding the Day of the Lord.

> The Temple of your God has been deprived
> of the grain offering and the drink offering …
> Alas for the day!
> for the Day of the Lord is at hand,
> coming as destruction from the Almighty.
> - Joel 1:13-15

The prophecy of the loss of 'the grain offering and the drink offering' was not completely fulfilled in Old Testament times. We know this because Joel was prophesying events far in the future, in the end times, when 'the Day of the Lord is at hand.' The loss of 'the grain offering and the drink offering' corresponds to the 'abolition of the daily sacrifice' referred to repeatedly in Daniel and by Jesus in the gospels, and its replacement by the abomination of desolation, a fake eucharist.

This prophecy in Joel draws a link between the loss of the Eucharist and the Day of the Lord. When the Eucharist is abolished and replaced with a blasphemous alternative, the Day of retribution will be at hand. This supports what we've been saying about the Eucharist being at the center of God's plans. It is at the center of God's purpose in creating a material universe and a race of embodied spirits. The purpose is Christ. The purpose is God's desire to give himself to his creature in all the fullness of his own Godhead, which he cannot do spiritually; he can only do it bodily.

Take away the Eucharist, rob God of his desire to give himself to his people Eucharistically, and the provocation has reached its full extent. God will no longer hold back his hand. Take away the Eucharist and the retribution is about to fall on the earth. This is the meaning of Joel's call to the priests to lament the loss of the grain offering and the drink offering.

The extended description of the Day of the Lord in Joel 2 corresponds in great detail to the description in Ezekiel 38, though it doesn't list the nations that will come against Israel.

> Blow the ram's horn in Zion,
> sound the alarm in my holy mountain:
> let all the inhabitants of the land tremble:
> for the Day of the Lord is coming,
> yes, it is near at hand.
> A Day of darkness and gloom,
> a Day of clouds and thick darkness,
> like the dawn across the mountains
> spreads a vast and mighty horde,
> such as has never been seen before,
> such as will never be again
> to the remotest ages.
>
> - Joel 2:1,2

The closing lines of verse 2 reflect what Daniel says, repeated by Jesus in the gospels, about days of distress such as have never been before and never will be again. The account is filled with expressions which can easily be cross referenced to other prophecies in Scripture about the Great Day.

> A fire devours before them,
> and behind them a flame burns,
> the land is as the garden of Eden before them
> and behind them a desert wilderness,
> and nothing shall escape them.
> — Joel 2:3

The 'garden of Eden' language mirrors the description in Ezekiel 38:11 of 'this peaceful nation living secure.'

> Like chargers they gallop on ...
> At the sight of them, people are appalled,
> and every face grows pale ...
> they never jostle each other,
> each marches straight ahead ...

They hurl themselves at the city,

they leap onto the walls, climb upon the houses,

and enter in windows like thieves.

- Joel 2:4-9

The Lord then intervenes suddenly. Every line in the description now mirrors the language in other prophecies of the Day.

As they come on the earth quakes *(Ezekiel 38:19)*;

The skies tremble,

sun and moon grow dark *(Isaiah 24:23)*,

the stars lose their brilliance *(Ezekiel 32:7)*:

Yahweh's voice rings out

at the head of his troops *(Psalm 46:6)*,

for mighty indeed is his army,

strong the enforcer of his word,

for the Day of Yahweh is great and very terrible,

and who can face it? *(Revelation 6:17)*

Joel 2:10,11

The Day of the Lord Draws Closer

Joel goes on to speak words of comfort to those who place their trust in the Lord, just as Jesus later reassures his disciples and tells them to have no fear, because when they see these things beginning, it means that their liberation is at hand (Luke 21:28).

'Land, do not fear, be glad and rejoice, for the Lord will do great things,' he tells them (Joel 2:21). 'I will restore to you the years that the locust has eaten' (Joel 2:25).

The Day of the Lord will be followed by a time of great restoration, when 'your sons and daughters shall prophesy, and your old men shall dream dreams' (Joel 3:1).

The later verses of Joel emphasize Yahweh's kingship centered in Jerusalem. One effect of the Great Day will be to establish Jerusalem as the place from which Christ reigns, and to make known to his people that he is their Messiah, the one who saves them, the one who rescues them from all their enemies.

After the Great Day, Jerusalem will no longer be 'trampled by Gentiles' as Jesus expressed it (Luke 21:24). The Day of the Lord will result in the Gentiles recognizing the distinct identity of the Jews and their right to remain in possession of their God given land, the land of Israel.

When 'the times of the Gentiles will be fulfilled' (Luke 21:24), Gentiles will no longer claim any rights over the land of Israel, because all Gentiles will at last acknowledge without reservation their debt to the Jewish people from whom their Savior also comes.

> Yahweh roars from Zion,
> he thunders from Jerusalem;
> heaven and earth tremble ...
> then you will know that I am Yahweh your God
> dwelling in Zion, my holy mountain.
> Jerusalem will be holy
> and no foreigners will ever overrun her again.
> - Joel 4:16,17

As Ezekiel never tires of pointing out, the recognition of who Christ is, the knowledge of God in Christ, will resolve all conflict between Jews and Gentiles. 'And they will know that I am the Lord.' When that happens, when both Jews and Gentiles receive the knowledge of God, that he is the one made manifest in Christ, the world will be at peace, and the peace will endure from century to century.

HABAKKUK

Every line of Habakkuk's description of the Day of the Lord is worthy of close attention. His vivid account is densely packed with information. The impact his vision has on his own spirituality, and which it is meant to have on ours, is described with a precision one finds in no other prophet.

As mentioned in the Introduction to this work, the Book of Habakkuk begins with an agonized conversation with God, in which the prophet wants to know how God can appear to stand idly by while his people are being molested and harried and even destroyed by hard hearted peoples bent on no greater purpose than the frivolous desire to enlarge their own wealth.

God answers Habakkuk. He is not standing idly by. He is working out his own purposes for his people. Those who come against them look like the victors but their victory rests on no good foundation. They will themselves be quickly destroyed just as they have destroyed. It is all known by God and provided for in advance by him.

> Then Yahweh answered me and said,
> 'Write the vision down, inscribe it on tablets
> to be easily read.
> For the vision is yet for an appointed time,
> but in the end it will speak, and will not lie:
> though it tarry, wait for it,
> because it will surely come, before too long.
> Behold, anyone whose soul is unrighteous will
> succumb,
> but the righteous will live by faith.'
> - Habakkuk 2:2-4

God tells Habbakuk to write the vision down 'on tablets' when he receives it. He is telling him that he wants the vision to be included in Scripture. It will not be a lie. It will not be given in vain. It will be divine truth which everyone needs to know about.

God then adds several comments about the length of time it will take for the vision to come and to be realized. It will 'tarry,' it will be a long time in coming, but we are to wait for it. We are not to forget about it. The vision is given to us as knowledge of the highest importance, and it will surely come at its appointed time.

God then makes it clear that the vision will be so overpowering that those who are not well prepared will be upended by it. They will go under. Those who live by pride in themselves will not be able to withstand the vision. It will destroy them. But those who live by faith in Yahweh their God will have the foundation strong enough to stand firm in the Day of ordeal.

God is telling us here through his prophet Habakkuk that the Day of the Lord, and the advance knowledge of it given to us by the prophets, stands as our test. If our souls are not true, if we have not learned to trust in the only true Lord and build our foundations on him, the test will find us wanting. We will deny the vision, or ignore it, or try to explain it away with glib talk. We are not yet ready to stand in the presence of the full truth given to us in the word of God.

Only when we have matured in faith, having learned by hard experience to place all our hope only in our King, our Savior, our Christ, will we be able to face the full truth contained in the prophecies of the Day of the Lord and not fall back.

When the vision of the Day of the Lord comes to Habakkuk it gives him the shock of his life, bringing an end to all his arguments and, when he has recovered from the shock, bringing far greater satisfaction to his spirit than he could ever have imagined before he received it.

That is the mysterious thing about the Day of the Lord. The prophetic descriptions of it are terrifying. Yet for those who have learned that he is their only Healer and their only Savior, the knowledge of it brings deep peace to the spirit.

After Habakkuk has seen the vision, he understands. The day of disaster does indeed strike for God's people, but only to clear out their confusion, only to dispel their double mindedness. It brings them swiftly into a true relationship with their Savior God. They learn to trust in him alone, and to receive him into their spirit at a depth they never dreamt of before. God uses the day of disaster to lift them up to the high places where they at last receive the knowledge of the only true God, made manifest in the only true Christ.

In this short Book of the Bible, Habakkuk tells us of the intense wrestling he himself engaged in, in connection with the vision given to him of the Day of the Lord. In giving us his intimately personal and totally honest account of how he 'wrestled' with God and dealt with his vision, he also gives us deep truth not only about what the Day of the Lord will look like, but on what God means by telling us about it in the first place, and telling us about it so insistently, so repeatedly. More than any other prophet, Habakkuk gives us a window into understanding why God keeps returning to this subject throughout the scriptures.

In reading Habakkuk's account it becomes clear that God gives us so much information about the Day of the Lord, and repeats himself so often, because he wants all of us, including all those who will not be on this earth when the Day comes, to know about the Day, and to be challenged by it, and to find our way to overcome the challenge.

This, I feel, is why the text even seems to blur the distinction between the Day itself and the vision Habakkuk will receive of the Day. 'The vision is for its appointed time ... although it may tarry, wait for it, for come it certainly will before too long' (Habakkuk 2:3). What will tarry, the prophet's vision of the Day or the Day itself? What will come before too long, the prophet's vision of the Day or the Day itself? I am not certain, the text doesn't say, and in any event I am not sure it matters. Habakkuk received the shock of his life from the vision, thousands of years before the Day which has not yet occurred even as I write this.

And that's the point. It was God's purpose to impress Habakkuk strongly with what will happen on the Day, just as strongly as if he had lived through the events of the Day itself. By having the vision, he has already seen the Day.

That is the effect that all of the scriptures about the Day are meant to have on all of us.

Turning now to his account of the vision: He begins by confirming that when the Lord appears he will be coming from the direction of Arabia.

> God comes forth from Teman,
> the Holy One comes from Mount Paran.
> His majesty covers the heavens,
> and his glory fills the earth.
> - Habakkuk 3:3

Teman and Mount Paran are in Edom, the part of Arabia closest to Israel. How does his glory fill the earth, if he is coming to Mount Zion from the direction of Arabia? This question comes up frequently in end times prophecy. How, for example, can the whole world, people of every tribe, nation and language, stare at the corpses of the two prophets for three and a half days as recounted in Revelation 11:9,10, and rejoice over their deaths, and give each other presents?

It could happen miraculously, of course. When he comes to judge all the living and the dead on the Day of Judgment, we will all be gathered together and we will see him. When he comes on the Day of the Lord, on the other hand, the prophecies do not indicate that all the peoples will be gathered together into his presence. Yet his majesty will cover the heavens and his glory will fill the earth. The end times events will be seen throughout the world at the same time. How will it happen?

The only answer I can think of, apart from the possibility of the miraculous, is that information technology will allow the whole world to witness events simultaneously. We are close to being at that stage already. Events are known and seen around the world now within seconds of their happening. By the time the Day of the Lord arrives, this kind of communication may well be practically instantaneous, and received by everyone.

> His brightness is as the light.
> - Habbakuk 3:4

This confirms what Isaiah repeats three times about the Lord at the moment of his appearance, '... the brilliance of his majesty, when he arises to make the earth quake' (Isaiah 2:10, 2:19, 2:21).

In a further detail, Habakkuk places beyond doubt that what is described is an intervention by Christ appearing visibly in his risen body. In many other prophetic passages it is close to certain that this is what is prophesied. In this one, I believe it is certain:

> Rays flash from his hands;
> that is where his power is hidden.
>
> - Habakkuk 3:4

This tells us both that we are looking here at the risen body of Christ, and that his wounds will still be visible on his body when he appears on the Day of the Lord. Rays of light will be flashing from where the nails pierced his hands at his Crucifixion.

'That is where his power is hidden.' The authority and kingship of Jesus was given to him by the Father on account of his sacrificial self offering. 'He humbled himself even to accepting death, death on a cross. Therefore God has highly exalted him, and given him

The Day of the Lord Draws Closer

the Name which is above all names' (Philippians 2:8,9). The Cross is the source of our power. In the Cross is our victory and our salvation. This information is all contained in Habakkuk 3:4.

> When he stands up, he makes the earth tremble;
> with his glance, he makes the nations quake,
> and the eternal mountains are dislodged.
> - Habakkuk 3:6

'With his glance, he makes the nations quake.' This confirms that the detail in Ezekiel 38:18, about the Lord's fury rising up in his face, means that Christ will appear bodily on the Great Day.

The prophet goes on to ask if the Lord is angry with the rivers and the sea, they are in such turmoil. In the same verse he answers his own question. The Lord has weaponized his creation, as in the Book of Wisdom, making use of it to deliver his people.

> Yahweh, are you enraged with the rivers,
> are you angry with the sea,

> that you should ride upon your horses
> and your chariots of salvation?
>
>   - Habakkuk 3:8

The account then describes the warfare in terms similar to those used in other prophecies.

> You uncover your bow,
> give the string its fill of arrows,
> you drench the soil with torrents;
> the mountains see you and tremble;
> great floods sweep by, the abyss roars aloud,
> lifting high its waves.
> Sun and moon stand still in their dwellings;
> they flee at the sight of your arrows,
> at the flash of your glittering spear.
>
>   - Habakkuk 3:9-11

These verses can easily be taken as an account of the actions of Christ in the warfare, but it would be possible to interpret them symbolically as the actions of God making use of his creation. In the verses that follow, on the other hand, one would have to stretch the interpretation too far to read the physical actions as symbolism. They are a physical description of Christ acting in his risen body.

> In rage you stride across the land,
> in anger you trample the nations.
> You marched out to save your people,
> to save your anointed one;
> you wounded the head of the house of the wicked,
> laid bare the foundation to the rock.
> With your shafts you pierced
> the leader of his warriors
> who stormed out with shouts of joy to scatter us,
> as if they meant to devour
> some poor wretch in his lair;
> with your horses you trampled through the sea,
> through the surging abyss.
>
>   - Habakkuk 3:12-15

Habakkuk then turns to the effect that his vision has had on him, much as Daniel described his own reaction to the visions he had received (in Daniel 8:27, for example, where he describes himself as fainting and remaining ill for several days).

> When I heard, I trembled to the core,
> my lips quivered at the sound;
> my bones became disjointed
> and my legs gave way beneath me,
> but calmly I wait for the day of anguish
> which is dawning on the people who attack us.
>
> - Habakkuk 3:16

Peace in the face of great distress, this is the effect in the prophet's soul of the power of the Lord working in him.

He then envisages a time of material want, perhaps in the aftermath of the warfare, a time of natural disaster in which there will be crop failure, loss of all livestock, fig trees going barren, vines bearing no fruit.

These things do not drive him to despair. On the contrary, they only cause him to rejoice and exult all the more in the God who saves his people. The prophet is giving a lesson in the spirituality of the *via negativa,* the way of negation, when poverty of material goods leads by divine grace to the activation of the spirit and an in-pouring of the love of God.

> For the fig tree will not blossom,
> nor will the vines bear fruit,
> the olive crop will disappoint
> and the fields will yield no harvest;
> the sheep will vanish from the fold
> and there will be no herd in the stalls:
> yet I will rejoice in Yahweh,
> I will exult in the God of my salvation.
> The Lord my God is my strength;
> he will make my feet light as a hind's,
> he will set my steps on the high places.
> - Habakkuk 3:17-19

We cannot be certain whether this passage is intended by Habakkuk as part of the prophecy of what will happen, or a more general comment on personal spirituality along the lines we've discussed, a piece of counsel on how to turn adversity into an opportunity to draw closer to the Lord. I think it is more likely the latter as this passage does not match anything in the other biblical accounts of the Day of the Lord.

In any event, the passage brings good counsel to all, including to those who will not be alive on earth when the Day arrives. It instructs us on how to learn from the prophesies of the Day of the Lord even if we will never see it while we are in this world.

When crisis strikes in our personal life, we need to recognize the day of our testing, and cling all the harder to our Savior. We need to look beyond all appearances and know by faith that he is the one who leads us, he is the one who guides us to the high places, he is the one who, if we trust him through the darkness, will bind us to himself forever in a joy that cannot be described.

Habakkuk is telling us that the day when everything else fails us is the day on which our personal liberation has come; it is the day on which the grace of God in Christ is putting steel in us so that we can belong to him in purity and in integrity, and forever.

The Day of the Lord Draws Closer

Habakkuk is not the only prophet who integrated an account of his own personal struggle to understand, and to reach spiritual breakthrough, with his account of the Day of the Lord. Jeremiah also provides intimate records of his own wrestling with God. Daniel tells of the disturbing effect his visions of the future had on him. But for the most part, the prophetic accounts of the Day of the Lord are presented simply as prophecy, simply as a relating of a vision of future events.

Habakkuk, on the other hand, begins with his own personal struggle and ends with his own personal resolution, arrived at after his vision of the Day which comes in between and which has such a disturbing effect on him. Daniel simply stated that he fainted. Habakkuk describes what happened to him in much greater detail, saying that he trembled to the core, his lips quivered, weakness invaded his bones and his legs gave way beneath him, before he was led to the spiritual breakthrough that brought him deep peace and power to meet any adversity.

To come face to face with the full dimensions of what Christ will do on that Day is also to come face to face with our own immaturity in faith. If we have not really embraced the kingship of Christ; if we are still double minded; if we still believe in our inmost hearts that the rulers of this world have a stronger claim on our loyalty than Christ the King has; if we cannot make up our minds whether Christ or Belial occupies the throne in our soul; then that Day will overtake us like a thief even if we never see it other than in the biblical prophecies.

The biblical prophecies of the Day of the Lord compel us to face our own inadequacies, our confusion, our inability to confess Christ with a single voice and a clear conscience. That realization of inadequacy is the beginning of healing. It is a key step in the work which Christ wants to do in us when we realize that we have been building our house on shaky foundations.

How to find our way forward after we have received the shock of our lives from 'the vision' of the Day, that is what Habakkuk teaches us. The prophet who had most difficulty with it himself is – guess what? – the one who knows best how to guide us through the ordeal.

ZEPHANIAH

The whole of the Book of Zephaniah is taken up with the Day of the Lord. Its descriptions of the Day do not add much detail to the descriptions found elsewhere in Scripture. It is distinguished rather by the clinical accuracy of its diagnosis of root causes, by listing the groups of people who will be destroyed, by counseling on how the believers in the Lord may keep themselves safe during the crisis, and by indicating some of the results of the events of the Day.

Zephaniah 1:2-13

Those who will be destroyed are identified by their actions. They are those who ignore Yahweh, or hold him in contempt, or dedicate themselves to other gods.

> I will wipe out the remnant of Baal from this place,
> the very name of his priests,
> and those who worship the array of heaven
> upon the housetops.
>
> — Zephaniah 1:4,5

The Baal worshipers and the star worshipers, those who have gone wholly over to other gods, bringing a terrible curse on themselves and on their land, will be wiped out on the Day of the Lord. So will those who try to play it both ways, worshiping Yahweh, but swearing by foreign gods so as to make business deals run smoothly.

> … and those who prostrate themselves before
> Yahweh
> but swear by Milcom;
>
> - Zephaniah 1:5

This text offers a glimpse of life in Israel shortly before the Exile. Divided worship occurred in Israel as a result of trading with the surrounding peoples. The major trade routes led around Israel. The Silk Road ran westwards through Damascus and continued north of Israel to Tyre and Sidon; another branch ran southwards along the King's Highway to the east of Israel and on to Egypt. The Way of the Sea linked

Egypt with Tyre and Sidon along the west coast of Israel.

Israel's market towns were linked to these major routes by a network of roads extending throughout the country. When it came to striking a deal, a contest frequently arose over whose god to swear by in order to seal the deal. If a foreign dealer in a strong financial position insisted that his Israelite counterparty swear an oath by a foreign god, the Israelite might think it awkward to refuse.

Hence the disaster of divided loyalty among God's people Israel, under the pressures imposed in doing business with unbelievers. It was happening in Israel three thousand years ago. It remains the greatest challenge to God's people today.

Divided worship is even more hateful to God than outright idolatry. He wishes we were hot or cold, but if we are lukewarm he will spew us out of his mouth (Revelation 3:15,16). The famine that raged through the land in the time of Elijah was a result of this kind of two faced worship, calling Yahweh by the name of

Baal, and Baal by the name of Yahweh. Nothing infuriates God more quickly.

Those also who ignore the Lord are bringing themselves under a curse and will not survive the terrifying events of the Day of the Lord. We are called to thank and praise him for the things he does for us, and to call on him on the day of trouble. Those who have heard of him but do not call on him, do not thank and praise him, do not dedicate themselves to him, will have nowhere to turn when the crisis comes. God cannot help those who treat him as if he had nothing to do with them. The Day of the Lord will find them unprepared.

> … and those who have turned their back on Yahweh,
> who do not seek Yahweh
> and do not consult him.
>
> - Zephaniah 1:6

They are condemned again later in the chapter under the heading of the winebibbers:

> When that time comes
> I will search Jerusalem by lamplight
> and punish the men stagnating
> over the remains of their wine,
> who say in their hearts,
> 'Yahweh can do nothing either good or bad.'
>
> - Zephaniah 1:12

Zephaniah 1:14-18

This passage describes the Day of the Lord in terms already familiar. It is 'a day of darkness and gloom, a day of cloud and thick fog, a day of trumpet blast and battle cry ... the whole earth will be consumed by the fire of his jealousy.'

Zephaniah 2:1-3

The description of the Day is followed by a set of advance counsels on how the nations might be able to avoid the horrific events to come. Not everyone will be swept away in the destruction. The humble of the Lord, who keep his commandments, may find shelter on the Day of the Lord.

> Seek Yahweh, all you humble of the earth,
>
> who obey his commands;
>
> seek righteousness, seek meekness;
>
> it may be you will be hidden
>
> on the Day of the Lord's anger.
>
> — Zephaniah 2:3

These are the ones who have not worshiped false gods, have not worshiped the statue of the beast and have not accepted his branding (Revelation 20:4), those who keep the commandments of God and have in themselves the testimony of Jesus (Revelation 12:17).

Zephaniah 2:4-3:8

These verses begin with a list of some of the nations that will be affected in the destruction. They are, the land of the Philistines, Moab and Ammon, Cush, and Assyria. The list ends with Judah, and her capital Jerusalem, whose condition is diagnosed here in great detail.

The Day of the Lord Draws Closer

> Disaster to the rebellious, polluted, tyrannical city!
>
> She has not listened to the call,
>
> she has not bowed to correction,
>
> she has not trusted in Yahweh,
>
> she has not drawn near to her God.
>
> Her rulers are roaring lions,
>
> her judges are wolves of the wastelands
>
> that leave nothing over to the morning.
>
> Her prophets are braggarts, imposters,
>
> her priests have polluted the sanctuary
>
> and done violence to the Law.
>
>   - Zephaniah 3:1-4

This point by point critical report on Jerusalem and its leading men leaves nothing to the imagination.

 The passage ends with a brief description of the assembly of the nations against Israel and their destruction on the Day of the Lord.

> I am determined to gather the nations,
>
> to assemble the kingdoms,
>
> to pour upon them my fury,

all my fierce anger,

for the whole earth will be devoured

by the fire of my jealousy.

- Zephaniah 3:8

'Jealousy,' or zeal, is again emphasized. Here it is God's jealousy in regard to his people Israel and against their enemies. Our God is very jealous in regard to the people among whom he will be born, his family in the flesh. He will not tolerate for long those who come against them.

And neither will he tolerate for long any divided loyalty among his people. We are either for him or against him. We cannot belong in his kingdom as long as we cling to idols, as long as we give any credit whatever to his rivals in the demon kingdom who work ceaselessly to draw us onto their ground. 'Purify your hearts, you double minded (James 4:8).

All double mindedness needs to be driven out and will be driven out on the Day of his wrath. 'He jealously desires the spirit which he has made to dwell within us' (James 4:5). We can only be blessed by

The Day of the Lord Draws Closer

dedicating ourselves to him and to him alone. His enemies in the demon kingdom under Satan are incapable of giving us anything but destruction. That is why our God is so jealous in our regard. His jealousy, his zeal for the honor of his own Name, is our greatest defence. It is the reason for all our blessings. It is the reason for the things he will do on the Day of his wrath.

Zephaniah 3:9-20

The prophet now returns to the theme of encouragement, detailing at length the results of the Day of the Lord and inviting us to look forward eagerly to the renewed world that will emerge from it.

> Yes, then I will purge the lips of the peoples,
> that they may all invoke the name of Yahweh
> and serve him shoulder to shoulder.
> - Zephaniah 3:9

And Israel will be healed of her long years of unbelief, having experienced her true Messiah as her Warrior-Savior. The lips of 'the peoples' will be 'purged.' The names of false gods will not cross their lips again, and this will be true not only of the market towns of Israel under pressure from foreign dealers, because the lips even of the foreign dealers, 'the peoples,' will be purged. All will flee from the mention of other gods.

'Do not mention the name of any other god: let none ever be heard from your lips' (Exodus 23:13). Thus spoke Yahweh to his people through Moses. And again through Joshua: 'Do not utter the names of their gods, do not swear by them, do not serve them and do not bow down to them' (Joshua 23:7).

The God we worship is a jealous God. 'For the Lord, whose Name is Jealous, is a jealous God' (Exodus 34:14). Say this to most Christians now, and they will think you have misunderstood God's words, or that you are a religious extremist of some kind; but the point will become glaringly obvious to all the peoples of the world on the Day of the Lord, and will remain so in the centuries following.

(A brief note on a modern confusion of language: The terms 'envy' and 'jealously' are now used interchangeably. Up to a few decades ago, 'envy' meant being greedy for the things that belong to others, which of course is always a sin; 'jealousy' meant being resolute in holding onto the things that belong to oneself, which is a virtue unless it becomes disordered. God's jealous love for his people is the greatest protection we have; to call it a sin would be outright blasphemy. It becomes difficult to understand this when, for example, modern translations of the Bible translate 1 Corinthians 13:4b as, 'Love is never jealous.' The older English translations render this as, 'Love envieth not,' which of course is much more accurate. I find it helpful to keep an old as well as a new translation of the Bible to hand. The scholarship behind the new may be better, but the language of the old is sometimes a lot clearer.)

> Zion, have no fear, do not let your hands fall limp,
> Yahweh your God is there with you,
> the Warrior-Savior ...
> he will dance with shouts of joy for you
> as on a day of festival.
>
> - Zephaniah 3:16-18

The nations of the earth will all respect Israel and its borders. All will be united in the knowledge of God which is in Christ, when Israel recognizes Jesus as her true Messiah. All Gentile peoples will realize that salvation is of the Jews and will not disturb them or challenge their right to their God given land and their God ordained city again.

> At that time I will be your guide;
> at the time when I gather you all in
> I will give you praise and renown
> among all the peoples of the earth,
> when I restore your fortunes under your own eyes,
> says the Lord.
>
> - Zephaniah 3:20

Not only will the world will be a very different place after the Day of the Lord; the beautiful thing is, the world will recognize what makes the difference. All the peoples of the earth, Gentile as well as Jew, will at last know the difference between light and darkness, between death and life, between the horror of serving Shishak and the joy of serving the living God, between Christ and Belial.

HAGGAI AND THE EUCHARIST

The Book of the prophet Haggai contains a very brief prediction of the Day of the Lord.

> A little while now, and I will shake the heavens and the earth, the sea and the dry land. I will shake all the nations, and the treasures of all the nations will flow in, and I will fill this Temple with glory, says Yahweh Sabaoth. The silver is mine, and the gold is mine, says the Lord of hosts. The glory of this latter house shall be greater than of the former, says the Lord of hosts, and in this place I will give peace.
>
> - Haggai 2:6-9

This prophecy was part of an exhortation to the returned exiles to rebuild the Temple in Jerusalem, but like so many biblical prophecies, it was to be fulfilled more than once.

That this prophecy still awaited fulfillment in New Testament times is shown in the Letter to the Hebrews, where it is repeated with different emphasis:

> I am going to shake the earth once more, and not only earth but heaven as well. The words 'once more' indicate the removal of what is shaken, since these are created things, so that what cannot be shaken remains. We have been given possession of an unshakeable kingdom.   - Hebrews 12:26-29

After the Day of the Lord the glory of the new Temple, which exists in the Church, will surpass that of the old.

What does this prophecy in Haggai mean? The sacrifice of animals in the Temple no longer has any validity in New Testament times. So what can it mean to say that the glory of the new Temple will surpass that of the old?

It can only have reference to the sacrificial Lamb, which is the Body of Christ in the Eucharist.

But how will the glory of the Eucharist be greater after the Day of the Lord? The Eucharist, being Christ's Body, is surely the same yesterday, today and forever?

His Body will be the same after the Day as it was before it. What will change is the recognition of his Body in the Eucharist by all the peoples of the earth. Something will happen on the Day of the Lord that will cause all the peoples of the earth to recognize him in the Eucharist with new conviction and new power. He will not be ignored, or made light of. People will not approach the Eucharist with unconfessed sins. The Day of the Lord will bring an end to all that.

The Eucharist will be at the center of God's purposes in the Day of the Lord. I infer this not only from the texts just quoted from Haggai and Hebrews, but from the many references in the prophecies of the Day to the abolition of the daily sacrifice and the installation of the abomination of desolation in its place.

The Book of Daniel contains three separate prophecies of these two events (8:11-13, 9:27, and 11:31). There was a fulfillment of Daniel's prophecy in the time of the Maccabees, when Jerusalem and its Temple were being turned over to Greek pagan religion.

> On the fifteenth day of Chislev in the year 145 the king built the abomination of desolation on top of the altar of burnt offering. - 1 Maccabees 1:54

But this event did not exhaust the significance of Daniel's prophecy. Jesus repeated it as we see in Matthew 24:15 and Mark 13:14. We know from this that the prophecy was still to be fulfilled in the time of the gospels.

Indeed, he treats the installation of the abomination of desolation as the trigger for his disciples to make their escape, the immediate harbinger of the 'great distress, unparalleled since God created the world, and such as will never be again' (Mark 13:19).

We recall also that Joel prophesied the end of the grain offering and the drink offering immediately before the Day of the Lord (Joel 1:13-15), and with their disappearance, all 'joy and gladness' is 'cut off from the Temple of our God' (Joel 1:16).

If the prophecies of the abolition of the daily sacrifice and its replacement with the abomination of desolation are at the center of the prophecies of the Day of the Lord; if they are the sign that the terrifying events of the Day are at hand; then the Eucharist is at the center of these events as well.

These prophecies tell us that getting rid of the Eucharist and replacing it with a fake sacrifice to himself is at the center of Satan's purposes. When he appears to have succeeded in this aim, it will be time for the Lord to intervene.

Now if the Eucharist is the central target of Satan's efforts, and the central reason for the Lord's intervention, it has to follow that the restoration of the Eucharist is the most important result of the Lord's intervention. It is the key element in the renewal of the church.

It follows from this that the church after the Day of the Lord will be a Eucharistic church. The life of the church will spring from the Eucharist and will flow to the Eucharist with greater power than the church has ever experienced before.

This means that there will be some connection between the manner of the Lord's appearing on the Day and the renewed centering of the church on the

Eucharist after the Day. His appearance will be such as to restore all things in the church. There will be no more division between Protestant and Catholic, because Christians will eat, drink, sleep, breathe and live both the word of God and the Eucharist. These essential lungs, so to speak, of the church's life, will breathe without any conflict between the two.

Something in his appearing will cause all unnecessary argument to fall away. Everything interfering with the union between God and his people will fade out at his appearing on the Day of the Lord.

ZECHARIAH

Zechariah places Jerusalem at the center of his account of the Day of the Lord. As in Jeremiah 25, Jerusalem is the 'cup which will set all the nations reeling.'

> Look, I will make Jerusalem a cup to set all the surrounding peoples reeling (that will be in the time of the siege against Jerusalem). When that Day comes, I will make Jerusalem a stone too heavy for all the peoples to lift, all that burden themselves with it will be cut to pieces, though all the nations of the world will be massed against her. When that day comes, says the Lord, I will strike all the horses with panic and their riders with madness, and I will strike all the peoples with blindness, but I will keep watch over Judah. - Zechariah 12:2-4

God's people will recognize where their strength is coming from and will give him the glory for it, turning away from all idols. This is always the result of the experiences God leads his people through.

The Day of the Lord Draws Closer

> Then the rulers of Judah will say in their heart, 'the strength of the inhabitants of Jerusalem lies in Yahweh Sabaoth their God.'   - Zechariah 12:5

Watch what happens when they begin to give Yahweh the glory:

> When that day comes I will make the rulers of Judah like a brazier burning in a pile of wood, and like a torch of fire in a sheaf; and they will devour all the peoples round about, to the right and to the left.
>   - Zechariah 12:6

The Lord, the Warrior-Messiah, begins to give his people victory over those attacking them.

> Yahweh will first save the tents of Judah ... When that Day comes, Yahweh will defend the inhabitants of Jerusalem; and the frailest of them will be like David.   - Zechariah 12:8

The Day of the Lord Draws Closer

When the Lord has destroyed the power of all the armies attacking Jerusalem, the inhabitants of Jerusalem, and then all the inhabitants of Israel, will begin to recognize who their Savior is, that he is 'the one whom they have pierced.' That recognition will be utterly transformative. It will utterly change the lives and the history of the Jewish people.

> When that Day comes, I will set about destroying all the nations who advance against Jerusalem, but over the House of David and the inhabitants of Jerusalem I will pour out a spirit of grace and prayer, and they will look at me. They will mourn for the one whom they have pierced as for an only Son, and weep for him as people weep for their firstborn. When that Day comes, the mourning in Jerusalem will be as great as the mourning for Hadad Rimmon in the Plain of Megiddo, and the country will mourn family by family.
> — Zechariah 12:9-12

The Day of the Lord Draws Closer

The detail in this intimate and moving account of the effect Christ will have on his people when he comes among them as their Savior, is unique among the Old Testament prophecies of the Day of the Lord. It is more than a clear and certain confirmation that Christ will appear bodily on the Day of the Lord. It is also an unambiguous confirmation that the conversion of the Jews to faith in Christ will take place as a result of his appearance on that Day.

Zechariah's prophetic account takes us right inside the experience his people the Jews will have on that Day. 'If their rejection meant the reconciliation of the world, do you know what their re-acceptance will mean? Nothing less than life from the dead!' (Romans 11:15).

'They will mourn for the one whom they have pierced.' It couldn't be clearer from this expression that the Messiah Savior of Israel is Christ, and that his people the Jews will at last recognize him for who he truly is 'when that Day comes.'

Zechariah was not content to restrict himself to an account of the Warrior-Messiah going forth and wreaking destruction on the enemies of his people. He doesn't omit that. He makes no attempt to skirt around the terrifying events of the Day of the Lord.

But he has the purpose in his sights all the time. The purpose is to lead Israel, his people in the flesh, to recognize him for who he truly is. His purpose will be fulfilled only when their hearts melt with the recognition that he is the one who gave his Blood for them.

When their Warrior-Messiah exercises his divine power to rescue them from the vast hordes of their enemies, then they will understand. Then they will recall the tender words with which he addresses them through Isaiah, that he was wounded for our sins, that by his wounds we are healed. Then they will know that their Warrior-Messiah is the one who made himself so vulnerable in their sight, the one they had pierced.

Then they will know that in the Blood of his Cross is their only hope, their only salvation, the only

The Day of the Lord Draws Closer

foundation of their restoration, the only power by which they can see the face of God and live.

'And then they will know,' as Ezekiel never tires of repeating, 'that I am the Lord;' that El is Yah, as Elijah proclaimed by his very name; that the Most High God is Yahweh of Israel; that Yahweh of Israel is Jesus, the one whom they pierced, the one who draws so close to them that his Blood is their very life.

Zechariah reveals the most intimate significance of the Day of the Lord for the Jewish people.

> When that Day comes, a fountain will be opened for the House of David and the inhabitants of Jerusalem to wash away sin and impurity.   - Zechariah 13:1

This is the fountain of mercy opened up by faith in the Blood of Jesus. 'There is a river whose streams give joy to God's city' (Psalm 46:4).

What sin and impurity will be washed away first? The sin and impurity of idolatry, the sin and impurity which Israel had fallen into from earliest times, the sin and impurity that brought the people of Israel under a curse time and time again throughout their history. This is the spiritual fornication, which is always followed by fornication in the flesh and by all manner of trouble.

> What that Day comes, says the Lord of hosts, I will cut off the names of the idols from the land, and they will never be remembered again; and I will also rid the land of the prophets, and of the spirit of impurity.   - Zechariah 13:2

Note in this verse, the spiritual impurity is rooted out first ('the names of the idols'), then the Lord will rid the land of impurity in the flesh.

The text in Chapter 14 alternates between further short descriptions of the Day of the Lord and details of the new heaven and the new earth, the unending Day which will follow the Final Judgment at the end of the world, which is more fully described in Revelation 21 and 22.

Zechariah 14 presents us with a difficulty. It is not clear whether the references to the Day of the Lord in this chapter are further elaborations of the Day

The Day of the Lord Draws Closer

described in Chapter 12, or whether they refer to a later battle immediately before the end of the world, similar to the description of a short, final conflict in Revelation 20:7-10.

There is little to indicate that the events prophesied in Zechariah 14:1-5 are distinct from the main Day of the Lord described in Chapter 12, but there are two things which point toward the possibility that this passage refers to a second conflict.

First, it comes immediately before the declarations that there will be 'one continuous day' with 'no more day and night' (14:7); that 'living waters will issue from Jerusalem' (14:8); and that 'the curse of destruction will be abolished' (14:11). These expressions all anticipate the terms used in Revelation 22 to describe the world after the Final Judgment and the close of the age, when the new heaven and the new earth will have been established.

Second, Zechariah 14:1-5 includes this:

I will gather all the nations to Jerusalem for battle. The city will be taken, the houses plundered, the

> women ravished ... Then the Lord will go forth and fight against those nations as once he fought on the Day of battle.   - Zechariah 14:2,3

'As once he fought on the Day of battle.' It is difficult to read this as anything other than an indication that we are looking at a second battle taking place long after the first one, when the first one has already become a distant memory. The point is not certain, but there are some indications at least that Zechariah speaks of a second conflict which will take place before the end of the world.

If it is true that Zechariah prophesied a second time of conflict, taking place immediately before the end of the world and long after the main Day of the Lord, then he appears to be the only prophet in the Old Testament who anticipated the second day of conflict in Revelation 20:7-10.

But again, the point is not certain because timescale seems to get jumbled in Zechariah 14. Even when he uses the language of Revelation about the new heaven and the new earth, he mixes it with texts which indicate that we are still in the present age when those nations that fail to come up to Jerusalem to worship on the Feast of Tabernacles will be punished with plagues (Zechariah 14:16-19).

The question whether there will be a further and final conflict immediately before the Second Coming is therefore not conclusively resolved in Zechariah 14. We will discuss this question in greater detail in a later chapter in relation to Revelation 20:7-10.

THE GOSPELS

In his prophetic comments about the end times, Jesus did not emphasize his role as the Warrior-Messiah marching out to defend his people on the Day of the Lord. He referred to the Day of the Lord in code, using some of the Old Testament expressions about lightning and the huge feast for the birds of prey, but it did not figure prominently in his teaching.

What he emphasized first in speaking about the future was his suffering and death, followed by his Resurrection, which would take place in Jerusalem. He prophesied these events to his disciples three times, and he did it spontaneously. He was not responding to questions from them. His words fell on deaf ears, yet he repeated three times that when they reached Jerusalem he would be handed over to the authorities there, and would be treated shamefully, would be scourged and crucified and would rise again from the dead on the third day.

His second concern was to lead his disciples to a sense of their mission and to let them know that it would begin soon, after he was taken away from them.

When he did come to speak about the end times, he didn't do it spontaneously; it was in response to a question from his disciples. And even when he did speak about the end times, it was to advise them on how to act rather than to feed their curiosity. He wanted to set their focus firmly on the Great Commission to go forth and spread the good news to the farthest corners of the earth; only then would he speak of the end times.

> "This good news of the kingdom will be proclaimed to the whole world as evidence to the nations. And then the end will come." - Matthew 24:14

A puzzling feature of his discourse is Jesus' repeated predictions that all the end times prophesies would be fulfilled in the lifetimes of at least some of his listeners.

> For the Son of Man will come in the glory of his Father with his angels, and then he will reward every

> man according to his works. In truth I tell you, there are some standing here who will not taste death before they see the Son of Man coming with his kingdom. - Matthew 16:27,28

This is clearly a prophecy of the end of the age, the Final Judgment leading into the new heaven and the new earth. Two thousand years after he said it, it still hasn't happened, yet Jesus told his disciples that there were some of them standing there who would see it in their own lifetimes.

The same prophecy is made in Mark 9:1. In Luke he prophesies the end times right up to and including the Final Judgment, and then declares that it will all have happened in the lifetime of 'this generation.'

> "In truth I tell you, before this generation has passed away all will have taken place." - Luke 21:32

When the high priest adjured Jesus, during his trial, to say whether he was the Christ, Jesus answered:

> "It is you who say it. But I tell you that from this time onward you will see the Son of Man seated at the right hand of the power and coming on the clouds of heaven."   - Matthew 26:64

We cannot impute to Jesus a lack of knowledge about the future. His prophecies are completely authoritative. We can only ask what he meant when he told his hearers that the end of the world would come in their lifetimes.

To understand what he was saying, I believe we need to make a distinction between the doing and the happening, the cause and the effect, the accomplishment and the taking place. The end of the world really was accomplished when Christ gave himself up in sacrifice on Calvary and rose from the dead on the third day.

Three words from his lips help us to understand this. In John's account, the last words he spoke before giving up his spirit to the Father were:

> "It is finished."   - John 19:30

It's been done. It's been accomplished. The whole of the Old Testament has been fulfilled, and the whole of the New Testament too. Nothing more is needed. Every good thing that ever has happened and that ever will happen 'comes down from the Father of all light' (James 1:17) by means of what was accomplished by the sacrifice of Christ on the Cross.

The Blood of Jesus is the cause of every gift we have. 'By his wounds you have been healed' (Isaiah 53:5). Isaiah made this declaration about six hundred years before the death of Jesus, but he uses the past tense. Every good thing that will happen throughout the history of the church, even before it has happened, has already been accomplished. The Blood of Jesus has accomplished it.

This is sometimes experienced by people who need to be healed from sickness. Their faith tells them they are healed, and they know they are healed, even while the healing has not yet fully manifested and they are still troubled by the physical effects of their sickness. The truth is that their healing has already been done by

Jesus even before it becomes manifest in time, in experience.

Those who still need to break loose from their sins sometimes feel assured that they have already been saved. They need to break with sin, this is absolutely indispensible, but while they are still aiming at victory an encouraging assurance may drive them on because, with the dawning of hope, they feel assured that the future is good because their redemption has already been secured by the Blood of their Savior. It has been accomplished even before they themselves have got over the line so to speak.

Someone may tell me that I'm interpreting Scripture according to my own wishes when I draw a distinction between the accomplishment by Jesus on the Cross, and the eventual outcome in historical time. After all, the phrase used in Luke 21:32 and Mark 13:30 is, 'before all these things have taken place.'

Or is it? I wish I had the scholarship to examine what Jesus originally said in his own language. Some older translations of the Bible are helpful toward making the distinction we need to make. They render the expression in Mark 13:30, 'till all these things <u>be done</u>.' And in Luke 21:32, 'till all be fulfilled.'

'Till all be fulfilled.' Now take a look at the older translations of Jesus' last words in John 19:30: "It is fulfilled." If 'fulfilled' is the word used by Jesus both on the Cross and in the end time prophecy in Luke 21:32, then the point is established: because in Jesus' mind, his sacrifice on the Cross is the entire fulfillment of the Old Testament, and it is the entire accomplishment of everything in salvation history, including the events still to take place.

"It is fulfilled." "It is done." Nothing more is needed. The life, death and Resurrection of Jesus fulfills everything in the Old Testament and accomplishes everything still to take place in the end times. This, to my understanding, is why Jesus told his disciples they would see the whole of salvation history being accomplished in their own time.

In Jesus' major end times prophecies in Matthew 24, Mark 13 and Luke 21, it is not immediately obvious that he makes any reference to the Day of the Lord at all. We need to pay close attention to see that his account of the Day of the Lord is separate from his account of the Second Coming at the close of the age. There are two different discourses, but it is easy to miss the distinction.

In Luke the distinction is made clearer because he has a separate section describing the time of the Day of the Lord in Chapter 17. In Matthew and Mark you may not notice the distinction unless you are looking out for it, because the prophecy of the Day of the Lord is placed alongside the prophecy of the close of the age. In all three accounts, Matthew's, Mark's and Luke's, Jesus begins with a warning about deception in regard to false Christs.

> "Many will come using my name and saying, 'I am the Christ,' and they will deceive many."
>
> - Matthew 24:5

In Luke's account, one mark of the times of the Day is that people will long to see 'one of the Days of the Son of Man.'

> "A time will come when you will long to see one of the days of the Son of Man and will not see it. They will say to you, 'Look, it is there!' or, 'Look, it is here!' Make no move; do not set off in pursuit."
>
> - Luke 17:22,23

Jesus then immediately makes it clear that he is speaking of the Day of the Lord by using the language of the prophets in regard to that Day:

> "For as the lightning flashing from one part of heaven lights up the other, so will be the Son of Man when his Day comes. But first he is destined to suffer grievously and be rejected by this generation."
>
> - Luke 17:24,25

Again, as so often, Jesus wants to bring the attention of his disciples to the crisis that will soon be upon them, the 'scandal' of the Cross; the end times will come later. Jesus closes this discourse with another expression that links it with the account of the Day of the Lord in Ezekiel and Revelation and some of the other prophecies:

> "Where the body is, there will the vultures be gathered together."   - Luke 17:37

Whereas in Luke, this account of the Day of the Lord occurs in a separate chapter from the one describing the Second Coming of our Lord at the close of the age (Chapter 21), in Matthew the account of the Day of the Lord is presented side by side with the account of the Second Coming.

Matthew, like Mark, shows Jesus speaking of the abomination of desolation and the pollution of the holy place, then speaking of the 'time of great distress, unparalleled since the world began, and such as will never be again' (Matthew 24:21). He then utters a second and elaborated warning about false Christs before referring to the Day.

> "If anyone says to you then, 'Look, here is the Christ,' or, 'over here,' do not believe it; for false

Christs and false prophets will arise and provide great signs and portents, enough to deceive even the elect, if that were possible. Look, I have given you warning. If, then, they say to you, 'Look, he is in the desert,' do not go there; 'Look, he is in some hiding place,' do not believe it; because the coming of the Son of Man will be like lightning striking in the east and flashing far into the west. Wherever the corpse is, there will the vultures be gathered together."

- Matthew 24:23-28

The lightning flashing and the vultures gathered around corpses are described together here. In Matthew's account, the end of the world is described in the verses immediately following, when the Son of Man will come in the clouds in power and great glory with his angels to gather the elect 'from one end of heaven to the other.' Matthew doesn't bracket out the account of the Day of the Lord and put it in a different chapter as Luke does; in Matthew, the two events, the Day of the Lord and the Final Judgment, are described distinctly but side by side. In both Matthew and Luke, however, it is clear that they are two different events.

The warnings about false Christs are dominant in all three accounts, and especially in Matthew. Our Lord is always, throughout Scripture and in all his dealings with us, very concerned that we keep ourselves protected from deception concerning his identity. Our need to know who he is is the deepest need in us. The wicked spirits will always try to mimic him in order to win our allegiance and so separate us from our Savior.

Jesus' end times discourses are filled with advice on how we, as individuals and as the church, need to act in regard to the events predicted. Jesus is never simply satiating curiosity. He always speaks life giving teaching about the demeanors we need to adopt and the actions we need to take if we are to survive the times of disaster. Every word of Christ is a saving word. His words don't bring mere entertainment or satisfaction of curiosity; they bring salvation. They are designed to change our thinking and affect how we act, as we can see in this example:

> "When you see Jerusalem surrounded by armies, then you must realize that it will soon be laid desolate. Then those in Judaea must escape to the mountains, those inside the city must leave it, and those in country districts must not take refuge in it. For this is the time of retribution when all that Scripture says must be fulfilled."   - Luke 21:20-22

This very practical advice was taken by his followers in the first fulfillment of the prophecy, the fall of Jerusalem in 70 a.d., when the Roman army razed the Temple and much of the city to the ground. The Jews who had not accepted Jesus' prophetic words remained in the city and fell in the carnage. Those who had heard and believed Jesus' advice fled before the onslaught reached the city, and so saved their lives.

This prophecy, in Luke 21:20-22, is a good example of a prophecy with layers of prophetic fulfillment. Jerusalem was surrounded by the armies of Rome in 70 a.d., the Temple was destroyed, the people of Jerusalem were scattered, and 'Jerusalem was trampled by Gentiles' for most of two thousand years, until the

Jewish people took possession of it again in the mid 1900s.

But these events do not exhaust the content of the prophecy. The destruction of Jerusalem in 70 a.d. does not wholly match the prophecy in Ezekiel 38 and 39 and the many other prophecies about the Day of the Lord. The nations listed by Ezekiel were not the nations coming against Jerusalem in 70 a.d. The Lord did not make a dramatic appearance to scatter the hostile armies and defend his people at that time either.

All of these elements of the prophecies of the Day of the Lord remain to be fulfilled, even after the partial fulfillment in 70 a.d. So when Jesus refers to 'the time of retribution when all that Scripture says must be fulfilled,' he cannot be referring to the Fall of Jerusalem in 70 a.d. alone. The complete fulfillment has yet to come.

To summarize: Jesus' advice in the course of his end times prophecies includes the following:

- He repeatedly tells us that we cannot know the date or the hour in which it will happen. That has not been revealed to us. It has been sealed in the heart of the Father. Any attempt to predict the time of the events prophesied is therefore bound to end in futility and embarrassment.

- He repeatedly warns against deception. We are to place our trust in him alone, and we are to pay no attention to anyone who claims to be the returned Christ.

- Jesus warns us to be ready at all times, because if we wait until the disaster is at the door, it will be too late. In Matthew 24:42-44, Mark 13:33-37, Luke 21:34-36 the message is the same: watch, keep yourself clean and in the grace of God, because you do not know the hour of your visitation.

- Don't be alarmed at the initial disturbances, the 'birth pangs,' or the 'beginning of sorrows,' because the end will not be yet (Matthew 24:6-8).

- Keep your eyes on the task to hand. The good news of the kingdom must be preached to all the nations first. This long term task is given to us to accomplish before the end will come (Matthew 24:14). On no account are we to hang around philosophizing about the end times and trying to predict when they will happen at the expense of the work we are called to do in spreading the good news of the everlasting kingdom of Christ.

- In telling us about the end times, Jesus is concerned to encourage and build us up, never to scare us away from the path on which he calls us. When we see these things begin to take place, he tells us to 'stand erect, hold your heads high, because your liberation is near at hand' (Luke 21:28). This message fills us with confidence, because we know that the result of the Day of Lord will be the complete renewal of the nations of the earth, when they will all be submitted to the kingship that will never come to an end, the kingship of Christ the Lord. We will not be troubled by persecution after these events take place.

With all of these provisos in mind, we can also affirm that all the elements of the other prophecies of Day of the Lord are present too in Jesus' prophecies. There will be a time of unprecedented disturbances in the world and in nature; there will be iniquity in high places, leading to the abomination of desolation and the celebration of a blasphemous pseudo eucharist; it will all be resolved when the Son of Man will come like lightning striking from east as far as west, and this will be followed by the liberation of the Church for the free and joyful practice of pure and true and faithful worship.

But before any of this, in Jesus' teaching, there is work to be done. There is a Faith to be built up. There is a kingdom to be established and spread. There is the work of God, 'that we believe in the one whom he has sent' (John 6:29).

2 THESSALONIANS

In 1 and 2 Thessalonians St Paul speaks of the end of the world and how the prophecies concerning the end times should influence present actions and demeanors.

He doesn't make a clear distinction between the Day of the Lord and the Second Coming. He rolls these two events into a single account of the end of the world.

His comments in 2 Thessalonians 2:1-12 elaborate on the earlier prophecies in Daniel and the gospels about what will happen in the lead up to the Day of the Lord.

His initial motivation in writing this passage is to calm his hearers down. They had become agitated as a result of discussing what he said in 1 Thessalonians 4:13-5:3 about the end of the world. They had picked up the impression that the end of the world was imminent and that they should now do nothing else but prepare for it. Some of them had even stopped doing any work and were encouraging others to give up working too.

His concern to correct their thinking, to protect them from deception, and to let them know that the Day of the Lord was still a long way in the future, led him to elaborate on all the things that must happen before the Day of the Lord can arrive. What he says shows us just how deeply imbued Paul's mind had been by the end times prophecies. There is some unique information in the passage.

> It cannot happen until the Great Revolt has taken place and there has appeared the wicked One, the lost One, the Enemy, who raises himself above every so called god or object of worship to enthrone himself in God's sanctuary and flaunts the claim that he is God. - 2 Thessalonians 2:3,4

This is the language both of Daniel 8:25 – 'He will challenge the power of the Prince of princes;' and of Isaiah 14:13,14 – 'higher than the stars of God I will set my throne ... I will rival the Most High.' In other words, what Paul envisages here is Satan, the spirit of Antichrist, coming in a human form, perhaps by diabolic possession of a man; but Paul is also elaborating on those earlier prophecies, telling us more precisely how they will be fulfilled.

There will be a 'Great Revolt' or a 'Great Apostasy.' The wicked one will 'enthrone himself in the sanctuary and flaunt the claim that he is God.'

In Daniel's account, it is not clear if the man of iniquity will be a secular leader who will gain illegitimate power over the Church and its pastors, or whether if he will succeed in taking on the appearance of being the leading pastor himself.

Will the man of iniquity pass himself off as pope? Is that what St Paul means by saying that he will enthrone himself in the sanctuary?

We need to be extremely careful in interpreting this prophecy. The Church is the Body of Christ. The Church is the Bride of Christ. She is indescribably holy, not because we her members are invariably holy, but because Christ himself inhabits his Church, and he certainly is invariably and indescribably holy. The sacraments of the Church are therefore indescribably holy. The offices exercised by the officers of the

Church are indescribably holy, and their ordination is indescribably holy.

Any suggestion that the Antichrist, Satan, will deceive his way into appearing to occupy the highest office of the Church and pass himself off as pope, even for a short, three and a half year period, is to be taken with great caution and to be discussed only with holy fear. If the thought of it lessens our reverence for the holiness of the Church we have missed the mark, because Satan targets the Church precisely because of her indescribable holiness, because the Church is the ark of salvation for all of us.

If this is what St Paul means by saying that the wicked One will enthrone himself in God's sanctuary, we need to bear the following in mind.

St Paul's words, which are very carefully chosen, make it clear that the Antichrist will not occupy the position of pope legitimately. He will 'enthrone himself in God's sanctuary,' and neither the office of a priest, nor of a bishop, nor of the pope, can be conferred on anyone by himself. It requires choice and an anointing by God. As Scripture teaches, 'No one can take this honor on himself; it needs a call from God, as in Aaron's case' (Hebrews 5:4).

It is therefore certain that the man of iniquity, the Antichrist, Satan acting by possessing a human being, will not become the validly ordained pope. But for a short period, the three and a half years immediately before the Day of the Lord, he will succeed in appearing to do so, and very many will be deceived. Very many will follow him.

Two points should be kept in mind here: First, the Day of the Lord will transform the church to greater glory than it has ever seen before; God will be praised in the Church's liturgies with a purity and a fullness that will be unprecedented after the purification of the Day of the Lord.

And second, the short, three and a half year period in which the Antichrist will appear to be in control, is, if my opinion is correct, a long way in the future, most likely centuries. Any suggestion that the Church is already in the crisis that will occur before the Day of the Lord is nonsense as I write this. And any diminishment of our belief in the holiness of the

Church and of the honor due to her ministers and of the necessity of her sacraments would be a total misreading of these biblical texts.

The exact opposite is the truth. The purification that will come for the Church on the Day of the Lord proves how holy the Church is, and how important it is to God that we understand the holiness of the Church.

And this is precisely the lesson we learn from the prophetic text in 2 Thessalonians 2:1-12. If we read these verses and conceive any hint of disrespect for the Church and its pastors, we've missed the point badly. The point is the lengths to which Christ will go to purify his Bride the Church and keep her holy.

The point is that when our enemy the devil directs all his energies and all his forces toward his attempt to degrade the Church, he is fighting a losing battle, and has been fighting a losing battle from the beginning, because Jesus has promised us that the gates of hell shall not prevail against the Church. They will surely throw everything they have into the attempt, but the attempt will fail.

The wicked One will 'enthrone himself in the sanctuary and flaunt the claim that he is God.' Note the clarity in Paul's language. The claim of the Antichrist that he is God is ridiculous; just as ridiculous is his self enthronement in God's sanctuary. This is an important point. Every bit as ludicrous as the wicked One's claim to be God is his enthronement of himself in God's sanctuary to pass himself off as the pope.

But however ridiculous the claim, however ludicrous the imposture, for a short time very many will be deceived by it. Daniel said of the man of iniquity that 'the Saints will be handed over to him for a time, two times and half a time' (Daniel 7:25). Revelation 13:14 tells us that the second beast, the beast like a lamb, will work miracles by which it will lead all the peoples of the world astray. Jesus tells us of times of great distress which, if they were not shortened, no human being would survive, a time in which signs and wonders would be worked by false christs and false prophets to deceive even the elect, if that were possible (Mark 13:19-22).

2 Thessalonians 2:4 looks like a declaration that the abolition of the daily sacrifice and the installation of the abomination of desolation will be accomplished by the Antichrist temporarily taking on the appearance of pastoral leadership of the church. From that position of fake leadership, he will, for a very short time, replace the Eucharist with a fake perversion designed to honor not God but Satan himself.

We don't need to wait for these events in order to learn everything we need to learn from them. The prophecies of the Day of the Lord in Scripture give us everything we need in order to learn these lessons, to be challenged by them, and to allow our faith to mature as a result of knowing about them. Like Habakkuk, we are profoundly shaken from 'the vision' of the Day even if we never get to see it; and 'the vision' drives us to place all our trust in the faithful and true witness who gives us all the strength we need to prepare for the ordeal.

Before he is destroyed by the breath of the Lord's mouth, the Antichrist will lead many astray. St Paul is here recounting the teaching of Jesus against deception.

> But the coming of the wicked One will be marked by Satan being at work in all kinds of counterfeit miracles and signs and wonders, and every wicked deception aimed at those who are on the way to destruction because they would not accept the love of the truth and so be saved. And for this reason God shall send them strong delusion, that they should believe a lie, so that all might be damned who did not believe the truth but had pleasure in unrighteousness. - 2 Thessalonians 2:9-12

The warning St Paul is giving us here is very similar to the warnings given by Christ. The root temptation in the 'times of great distress' is to abandon the faith in the truth, meaning to accept as Christ someone who is not Christ.

The 'deception' we are warned against is aimed at inducing us to practise idolatry, to worship a god who is not the true God, a god who rejects the true Christ and actually seeks to supplant him.

The prophecy of the coming of the Wicked One in 2 Thessalonians 2:3-12 is also a close match with the texts about the false prophet in Revelation 16:3, 19:20 and 20:10, which texts refer back to the second beast, the beast like a lamb in Revelation 13:11-17. Compare the latter text with the text from 2 Thessalonians 2 quoted above, and it becomes immediately clear that the same figure is referred to in each text.

The issue here is the issue that constantly comes up throughout Scripture: it is the issue of spiritual allegiance. Whom do you worship? In whom do you place your trust? Do you worship God, or do you make your sacrifice of praise to idols? Do you adhere to Christ, or do you allow yourself to be deceived into following Antichrist?

And St Paul, as always, draws the intimate link between faith in Christ and the power to do the works of righteousness. Those who are deceived are not deceived without cause. They are deceived into following false christs because they 'have pleasure in unrighteousness.'

St Paul is here drawing a clear distinction between those who are deluded by Antichrist and those who receive from God the power to stand firm. The ones who accept the love of the truth and do not take their pleasure in unrighteousness will be saved. They will not be deceived and will not follow the crowd into the Great Apostasy. The strong delusion will only come upon those who do not accept the love of the truth in Christ, those who take their pleasure in unrighteousness.

REVELATION

The Architecture

The Book of Revelation recounts a series of prophetic visions given to the apostle John concerning the future of the church. The events envisaged by John are not recounted in time sequence. They seem to follow each other in a sequence determined by a thematic logic, rather than according to a historian's concern with time. Time gets so jumbled in the Book of Revelation that it can be difficult to discern the logic in the sequence in which the visions are presented.

I count no fewer than seven separate accounts of the Day of the Lord in the Book of Revelation. Once we distinguish these accounts from the rest of the text it becomes easy to discern the architecture of the Book, which is designed around them. Each account emphasizes different features in the earlier biblical accounts of the Day.

The seven separate accounts are spread through the Book of Revelation from close to the beginning to close to the end. They are interrupted by passages some of which celebrate the great victory that will be enjoyed by the church after the Day of the Lord as if the Day had already passed; and some of which describe other, lesser disasters which do not bring the inhabitants of the earth to repentance.

The presence of seven accounts suggests that the Book of Revelation is taking up the theme of the Day of the Lord with a vengeance, so to speak. There have been earlier, very significant passages on the Day of the Lord in the gospels and in 2 Thessalonians; but in each of these cases the subject has been raised as a side issue, and in response to disciples' questions.

Jesus, in addressing these questions, is more concerned with the immediate future, his sacrificial death and Resurrection and the Great Commission to spread the kingdom throughout the earth. St Paul, in 2 Thessalonians 2, was forced to speak of the Day of the Lord by his audience, who had been foolishly expecting it to occur imminently.

Whereas Jesus and St Paul spoke of the Day of the Lord as a side issue, almost reluctantly, in the Book of

Revelation it is the central theme. It is the reference point for the other events in St John's vision.

The Book of Revelation was written later than the rest of the New Testament. The foundational doctrines of the faith had already been well established. The spread of the church throughout the world was already well under way. Now, the author felt free to speak of the end times without any need to restrain himself. He had no need to fear that his audience would overreact. There was no risk that they would lose sight of the truths of the gospel and the obligation to evangelize; no risk that the vision of the end times might lead Christians to lose focus and be seized with crazy ideas.

It looks likely that his new found freedom to speak of the Day of the Lord, so prominent a theme in the Old Testament, is one of the reasons St John provides seven descriptions of the Day.

There is one central description of the Day which serves as the focus for the rest of the Book, the point toward which it all moves, and from which the later events stem. This central account of the Day is the account, in Revelation 19:11-21, of the Rider and his armies, and the decisive victory he wins over the forces of Antichrist.

Revelation 19:11-21 is the climax of the Book, the point to which all the earlier events are leading, the point at which the action is most clearly narrated as present. There have been so many interruptions in the narrative, so many provisional descriptions of the Day, so many side shows so to speak, that when the Day comes into the mainstream of the narration in Revelation 19:11-21 it almost seems to be an anticlimax. One could say that we have been so well prepared for it by the passages leading up to it, that by the time it arrives, the impact it has on us as readers is weakened.

That feeling of a weakened impact, almost an anticlimax, is probably deliberate. For those of us who will not be alive when the Day actually happens, which is most of us, the preparation is all important. The Day itself is far in the future and affects us only through the advance vision we are given of it in Scripture.

That may be why St John is in no hurry to arrive at the climax. Like St Paul in 2 Thessalonians 2, and indeed like Habakkuk centuries before, St John also is concerned to let his readers know that, while the Day of the Lord should powerfully impact us in the present through the visions we are given of it in Scripture, the Day itself is not imminent. It will be a long time in coming. It will certainly come about in the appointed time, but don't be surprised if it should take a lot longer to arrive than we expected.

We will now take a look at the seven separate accounts of the Day of the Lord in turn, each of which describes part of the action, and all of which, when assembled together, comprise a complete account of the Day of the Lord prophesied in earlier scriptures.

The first occurs near the beginning of the Book:

> Behold, he is coming on the clouds; everyone will see him, even those who pierced him, and all the races of the earth will mourn over him. Indeed this shall be so. Amen. 'I am the Alpha and the Omega,' says the Lord God, who is, who was, and who is to come, the Almighty.   - Revelation 1:7,8

The Day of the Lord Draws Closer

The appearance of this passage at the beginning of the Book of Revelation is highly significant for the following reasons:

1. Its occurrence at the beginning of the Book serves to highlight the end result and the purpose of the Day of the Lord, which is that all the nations of the earth, Gentiles as well as Jews, should know who their true Lord is, the one whom they have pierced, the Christ, who loves them so intimately that his Blood becomes the foundation of their salvation and their lives. This end result and purpose is thus emphasized in the Book before any of the details of the Day of the Lord are given, preparing our minds for what is to come.

2. It confirms the prophecy in Zechariah 12:10,11, 'They will look on him whom they have pierced,' which is itself a very strong confirmation that Our Lord will make a visible appearance on the Day of the Lord in his risen body.

3. It extends the application of Zechariah 12:10,11 far beyond Israel to 'all the races of the earth.' All will look on him whom they have pierced and will mourn over him. While in Zechariah Israel alone is shown as

being drawn into repentance and a dramatic and decisive conversion to faith in Christ, here in Revelation 1:7 Israel's conversion is shown as being 'life from the dead' for all the Gentile peoples as well. All will realize that they are responsible for the wounds of Christ, the wounds by which they are healed.

4. Its occurrence in the Book of Revelation confirms that the prophecy of Zechariah is an end times prophecy, and its fulfillment was not exhausted when the St John cited it in relation to the Crucifixion (John 19:37).

5. It informs us at the very beginning that the visions in the Book of Revelation are not related in historical time sequence, as this consequence of the terrible events of the Day of the Lord is recounted in the Book's opening verses.

The second of our seven references to the Day of the Lord occurs in the sixth chapter.

In my vision, when he broke the sixth seal, there was a great earthquake, and the sun went black as coarse sackcloth; the moon turned red as blood, and the stars of heaven fell to the earth like figs falling from a fig tree when a mighty wind shakes it; and the heaven departed as a scroll when it is rolled together; and every mountain and island was moved out of its place. Then all the kings of the earth, and the rulers, and the rich men, and every bondman, and every free man, hid themselves in the dens and in the rocks of the mountains, and said to the mountains and rocks, 'Fall on us, and hide us from the face of him that sits on the throne, and from the retribution of the Lamb; for the great Day of his retribution has come, and who can stand before it?' - Revelation 6:12-17

This text declares itself as a description of the Day of the Lord; it uses similar terms to earlier biblical prophecies of the Day such as Isaiah 2:10,19,21, Isaiah 34:4, Joel 2:10 and Daniel 8:10.

The third description of the Day of the Lord occurs in the fourteenth chapter.

> The angel who had power over the fire left the altar and cried with a loud voice to the one that had the

> sharp sickle, 'Put your sickle in and harvest the clusters from the vine of the earth; for all its grapes are ripe.' So the angel set his sickle to work on the earth and harvested the whole vintage of the earth and cast it into the great winepress of the wrath of God, outside the city, where it was trodden until the blood that came out of the winepress was up to the horses' bridles as far away as sixteen hundred furlongs. - Revelation 14:18-20

This text uses the language of Isaiah 63:1-6 in describing the Day of the Lord – 'I have trodden the winepress alone.' It also uses similar language to Joel 4:13 – 'Come and tread, for the winepress is full; the vats are overflowing, so great is their wickedness.'

The fourth of the seven passages describing the Day occurs in the sixteenth chapter.

> Then there were flashes of lightning and peals of thunder and a violent earthquake, unparalleled since men came upon the earth. And the great city was divided into three parts, and the cities of the nations

The Day of the Lord Draws Closer

collapsed; Babylon the Great was not forgotten: God made her drink the full wine cup of his retribution. Every island vanished and the mountains disappeared; and hail with great hailstones fell from heaven upon the people, every stone about the weight of a talent.   - Revelation 16:18-21

The language is familiar from Ezekiel 38:19-22 and other scriptures prophesying the Day. Note here that whereas the cities of the nations collapsed, including Babylon the Great, the great city Jerusalem was not destroyed, only divided into three parts. The division into parts is described also in Zechariah 14:4,5.

Revelation 17 and 18, about the harlot of Babylon and her destruction, the fifth description, amount to an elaborate recounting of events forming part of the Day of the Lord. We will discuss it in a later chapter.

Revelation 19:11-21, about the deeds of the Rider and his armies, which is the sixth and the central description of the Day of the Lord in the Book of Revelation, will also be discussed later.

The seventh description of the Day of the Lord is the short one in the twentieth chapter.

> When the thousand years are over, Satan will be released out of his prison, and will come out to lead astray all the nations in the four quarters of the earth, Gog and Magog, to gather them together to battle, the number of them being as the sand of the sea. And they came swarming over the entire country and besieged the camp of the saints, which is the beloved City. But fire rained down on them from heaven and consumed them.   - Revelation 20:7-9

This passage uses the language of Ezekiel 38, but there are significant differences in setting. The description in Revelation 20 focuses on spiritual causation. 'Satan will be released out of his prison,' and he will 'lead astray all the nations in the four quarters of the earth, Gog and Magog, to gather them together for battle.'

The Gog in Ezekiel 38 is repeatedly specified as a particular human person in a particular place. He is 'the paramount prince of Meshech and Tubal' (Ezekiel

38:2, and 3, and 39:1, three times for emphasis), which are both located in what is modern Turkey.

By contrast with this specificity of person and place in Ezekiel 38 and 39, in Revelation 20:8 Gog and Magog are defined as 'all the nations in the four quarters of the earth.' They stand as symbols for all the rulers and all the nations of the earth. They will all be led astray by Satan and will all join with him in this warfare against God's people.

Is this a reference to a second Day of the Lord occurring later than the first and immediately before the Second Coming of Our Lord for the Final Judgment? There are grounds for believing that there will be such a second Day. We've seen that Zechariah 14:3 speaks of Yahweh marching out and fighting against the nations 'as when once he fought on the day of battle.'

There is also clear reference to time sequence at the beginning of the passage in Revelation 20:7: 'When the thousand years are over.' These are the thousand years of peace which will follow the Great Day described in Revelation 19:11-21. The conflict described in

Revelation 20:7-10 will take place after the thousand years and before the Second Coming.

There are thus good reasons to infer that there will be a second, short period of conflict before the end, and that this is what is referred to in Revelation 20:7-10.

And yet there are problems with this view. The problem that makes me reluctant to form the conclusion that there will be a second Day of the Lord is that, in spite of the differences alluded to above, the description in Revelation 20:7-10 remains a fairly close match to the description in Ezekiel 38 and 39; and the latter states very clearly: "This is the Day whereof I have spoken" (Ezekiel 39:8), leaving us in no doubt that the Day described in so much detail in Ezekiel 38 and 39 is the same Day described in the other biblical prophecies about the Day of the Lord, and that there will be only one such Day.

When we keep in mind the jumbling of time sequence that runs through the whole of the Book of Revelation, and when we remember that the description in Revelation 20:7-10 is the seventh of seven descriptions of the Day of the Lord spread through the

Book, it becomes equally reasonable to infer that the seventh is just one more description of the Day of the Lord recounted in the earlier six.

The seven descriptions of the Day of the Lord in Revelation comprise, when one adds them together, a complete account drawing on all the accounts of the Day of the Lord in earlier scriptures. None of the first six descriptions in Revelation uses the language of Ezekiel 38 and 39 about Gog and Magog leading all the armies of the earth in a vast campaign against Israel. The seventh description, the one in Revelation 20:7-10, fills in this gap by referring to Gog and Magog, and so completes the set of descriptions taken from earlier scriptures. This makes it very attractive to see it as a further description of the main Day rather then a description of a second conflict occurring much later.

But perhaps we don't need to make a choice between two mutually exclusive alternatives. Perhaps there is a third option. Perhaps there will indeed be a second conflict before the end, distinct from and less severe than the first, but otherwise looking like it. And perhaps the description of this conflict in Revelation

20:7-10 should not be applied solely to this second set of events, but should be taken both as one further description, the seventh of the seven descriptions of the principal Day, and also as a reference to the final short conflict.

I think this third one is the view I prefer, though I readily admit that there are also good grounds for adopting either of the first two. If we understand Revelation 20:7-10 as both a reference to a second conflict similar to the first and as a further set of particulars in the description of the first, we are easily able to understand Zechariah's account of Yahweh setting out to fight 'as when once he fought on the Day of battle' (Zechariah 14:3) as a reference to the second short conflict. Zechariah confirms with these words that the second short conflict is similar to the Day of the Lord, and he purposefully avoids confusing it with that Day.

However we resolve the difficulty, it remains true that if we put the seven separate prophecies together, what we have is a complete compilation of all the earlier prophecies of the Day of the Lord.

The Day of the Lord Draws Closer

The sequencing in the text appears random. As we've mentioned, events are recounted in an order determined by a thematic logic rather than in time sequence. And yet time sequence cannot be ignored. The history of the church takes place in time. We are moving from one set of events, described in the gospels, to another set of events, described in the prophecies of the end times. In the parable of the talents in Luke's gospel, Jesus explains the purpose of his going away in simple terms:

> He went on to tell a parable, because he was near Jerusalem and they thought that the kingdom of God was going to show itself then and there. Accordingly he said, "A man of noble birth went to a distant country to be appointed king and then return."
>
> - Luke 19:11,12

He was about to accomplish everything by his death and Resurrection. Nothing more would be needed, except that he must be appointed king, he must be established and recognized as king by all of his people; and that would be a complicated, painful and long

205

drawn out procedure. Just how painful, and complicated, and long drawn out is described in detail in the Book of Revelation.

What is the thematic logic we are speaking about? If the events in the Book of Revelation are sequenced according to theme rather than what is sometimes called 'linear time,' what is the theme, or what are the themes?

What we see in the Book of Revelation is a series of encouragements and of warnings, coming close on each other's heels. The Holy Spirit inspired John to write an account of the church's future which would both encourage the church toward the goal, and prepare the church for the ordeals it would meet on the way.

Frequently in the text, there is an outpouring in the heavenly community of loud, ecstatic praises of the Almighty for the victory he has already gained. On the Cross he has already gained the victory that is still to become manifest in the church's perilous journey.

That journey will see very many failures, and chastisements, and false starts, when the nations of the earth should have learned their lesson but didn't. This is necessary. It is necessary for all to understand that their salvation could never have come to them by any other means than the direct action of their Savior King, their Warrior-Messiah, their Lamb of Sacrifice.

We are looking at time from the perspective of eternity, and even in the midst of disaster here on earth, the choirs of heaven are singing the praises of the one who has already established his kingship and the salvation of his people. The text is shot through with so many rays of optimism and joy that we are spared from being driven to hopelessness by the dire events it describes.

These rays of optimism and joy survive through the accounts of the disasters through which the church will have to go. Nowhere in the Book are these disasters whitewashed. On the contrary, they are described in great detail and in the full dimensions of their horror. But we are never allowed to forget that the victory has already been gained, and that it belongs to Christ and to those who place their complete trust in him.

The letters to the churches in Chapters 2 and 3 also cause us to steady our vision, assuring us that the best preparation we can make is to deal with present challenges and to keep our robes clean as we wait in joy and confident hope for the appearing of the King. The churches addressed by Jesus in these two chapters are all in what is modern Turkey, the land of Meshech and Tubal from which Gog is to lead the armies of the nations against Israel on the Great Day.

Heaven then opens, and the apostle John is called up to see what is to take place in the future (Revelation 4:1). The passages which follow are filled with reassurance, as the armies of heaven sing praises to the Christ who has already gained his complete victory, and who alone is worthy to open the scroll containing the book of the future.

The breaking of the first six of the seven seals of the book is described in Chapter 6, at the end of which we have our third account of the Day of the Lord, discussed briefly above.

Chapter 7 is filled with the praise of God and the assurance of salvation to those who remain faithful.

Chapter 8 mentions 'the prayers of the saints' several times. These prayers are offered with incense by an angel on the altar of God. No hint is given about the effect of the prayers of the saints, whether the Day is to come as a response to these prayers, whether these prayers will hasten the coming of the Day, whether they will delay it, whether they will cause the time of retribution to be shortened.

Seven trumpets are given to the seven angels. The first six are sounded in Chapters 8 and 9, with descriptions of the disasters following.

Chapter 9 ends with a very significant passage:

> The rest of the people, who were not killed by these plagues, did not abandon the works of their hands and did not stop worshiping devils, the idols of gold, and silver, and brass, and stone, and wood, which can neither see, nor hear, nor walk. Neither did they repent of their murders, nor of their sorceries, nor of their fornication, nor of their thefts.
>
> - Revelation 9:20,21

A third of the people of the earth had lost their lives, but those who remained did not stop their idolatries, nor the fornication and child murder that always accompanies idolatry. These sins will continue to mount up until the seventh trumpet has been blown and the Day of the Lord arrives as it is described in 19:11-21. Only the direct, personal intervention of our Savior can give us the power to stop sinning.

Chapter 11:1-13 speaks of the two prophets. We will discuss this passage in a later chapter of this work.

In Chapter 11:15-18, the seventh angel blows his trumpet, there are shouts of triumph in heaven, with praise and worship and thanksgiving. The retribution is announced, the time has come, but the Lord does not appear yet. There is a delay. God grants a stay of execution so to speak.

First, the sanctuary of God in heaven opens and the ark of the covenant appears, accompanied by lightning, thunder, an earthquake and violent hail (Revelation 11:19). These details remind us of the descriptions of the Day of the Lord, but I don't count this passage among the seven descriptions of the Day in Revelation because it has a different function. It introduces Chapter 12 about the conflict between the woman and the dragon. This episode concerns events leading up to the Day rather than being part of the Day itself.

Chapter 12, the description of the conflict between the woman and the dragon, the Mother of God and Satan, will be discussed further later in this work.

At this point we might expect the Day of the Lord to be initiated by the seventh angel sounding his trumpet, but it is delayed. Perhaps the woman appealed for a delay until she had brought all her children into the kingdom. Perhaps the dragon requested more time to build up his armies. We are not told here.

Chapter 13 speaks of the dragon, the beast like a leopard, and the beast like a lamb. We will comment on these later.

Chapter 14 contains encouraging material about the companions of the Lamb alongside grim material announcing the fall of the harlot of Babylon.

Chapter 15 mixes the announcement of the final seven plagues with a hymn glorifying God and announcing that 'all nations will come and adore' him, following the manifestation of his acts of mercy.

In Chapter 16 the seven bowls of the seven plagues are emptied out over the earth. When the sixth angel has emptied his bowl, the time of the Day of the Lord is at hand. The call goes out from the three unclean spirits to all the rulers of the earth. They are to gather their troops together to the place in northern Israel called Armageddon for the final battle, which will decisively resolve the conflict between Christ and Antichrist.

> And I saw three unclean spirits like frogs coming out of the mouth of the dragon, and out of the mouth of the beast, and out of the mouth of the false prophet. For they are the spirits of devils, working miracles, who go forth to the kings of the earth and of the whole world, to gather them together for the war of the Great Day of God Almighty. Behold, I will come like a thief. Blessed is he who keeps watch, and keeps his garments on lest he walk naked and expose his shame. And they called the kings together to the place named in Hebrew Armageddon.
>
> - Revelation 16:13-16

The seventh angel emptied his bowl into the air, and the disturbances of the Day are shown coming over the earth in earnest, see 16:18-21, the fourth account of the Day in our discussion above.

Chapter 19 opens with a further song of praise before the main description of the appearance of the Lord on the Great Day.

Revelation 19:11-21 describes the Day of battle, the sixth in our list of the descriptions of the Day of the Lord. 20:1-6 describes the locking up of the dragon in the Abyss and the rule of the saints under Christ for a thousand years. 20:7-10 describes the battle which we have listed as the seventh account of the Day of the Lord. Chapters 21 and 22 describe the Final Judgment and the new heaven and the new earth which God will then bring forth.

We can see that the architecture of the Book of Revelation is an elaborate setting out of what happens while Jesus is 'gone to a distant country to be appointed as king and then return' (Luke 19:12). His kingdom is being prepared. His people are being purified. His enemies are being made a footstool for him to expand his kingdom to an extent which cannot be described, 'a great number that no man could count' (Revelation 7:9).

When he returns, his people Israel will at long last recognize that he really is their Messiah, and they will 'look upon him whom they have pierced and mourn for him as for an only child.' It will be the greatest reconciliation in history, 'life from the dead' as St Paul put it. And all those who were coming against Israel will recognize too that there is only one Savior, Christ the Lord. They will see that salvation is of the Jews and the most ancient hostility in history, anti Semitism, will at last be brought to an end.

The architecture of the Book of Revelation illustrates more clearly than anything else that Christ has been 'coming on the clouds of heaven with all his angels' from the time of his death and Resurrection. From our earthly viewpoint it takes an excruciatingly long time. From the viewpoint of eternity it all happens in a blink. 'He who testifies to these things says: I am indeed coming soon' (Revelation 22:20).

The Day of the Lord Draws Closer

In the following chapters we will take a look at each of Revelation chapters 11, 12 and 13. These three chapters provide a description of the spiritual condition of the world in the period leading up to the Great Day, a kind of extended diagnosis helping us to understand what needs to be remedied by the appearance of the Lord on that Day.

REVELATION 11

The Two Witnesses

What testimony were the two witnesses giving? The text in Revelation 11:1-13 doesn't spell it out. It does, however, tell us that the two witnesses were 'a plague to the people of the world' (Revelation 11:10).

Whatever their testimony was, it caused the people of the world to detest them. The nature of their testimony, though not specified, is indicated in the characterization of 'the great city' in verse 8.

> When they shall have finished their testimony, the beast that ascends out of the Abyss shall make war against them, and overcome them, and kill them. Their dead bodies shall lie in the street of the great city, which spiritually is called Sodom and Egypt, where also Our Lord was crucified.
>
> - Revelation 11:7,8

The city in which they will be killed is given three characterizations here. It is the city in which Our Lord was crucified, which of course is Jerusalem. It is also called symbolically or spiritually, Sodom and Egypt.

This means that the world in which God's people dwells will have fallen into widespread apostasy and corruption by two sins in particular: homosexual sin (Sodom) and idolatry (Egypt). It tells us that at the time of the Day of the Lord, the peoples of the world will have fallen away from their dedication to Christ and will have given their allegiance instead to demons through the sins of idolatry and sodomy.

They will be so far deceived in engaging in these two sins that they will regard the two prophets who testify against them as an utter nuisance, a 'plague' on the whole world. So great is their hostility toward the two witnesses, that when they are overpowered and killed by the beast, the people of the world will take to celebrating their deaths and giving each other presents (verse 10).

In earlier centuries this prophecy might have seemed far fetched. In our time, as I write this, it looks more like a statement of the obvious. Western nations, once dedicated to Christ, have been busy making laws in favor of the most abominable homosexual practices, and have been seeking to compel non western nations into following their lead and taking up this diabolical cause, enshrining in laws the delusion that homosexual practice is equivalent to the holy state of marriage, and imposing sanctions on anyone who voices disagreement.

The spiritual underpinning of this homosexual revolution has been the loss of all sense of the zeal and jealousy of God. Nations and their governments fall over themselves to honor every false religion, every false god, and to give no honor at all to the only true God, the only saving and healing God, the God who came among us in Christ. We even see the passing of laws prohibiting people from proclaiming the truth and refuting falsehood. Citizens in western countries get arrested for declaring Christian truth and warning against antichristian falsehood.

The principle is again proving true in the times we live in: The fall into spiritual fornication is always followed quickly by the fall into fornication in the flesh and every other manner of evil. A few decades ago these changes could not have been imagined. Now they have happened. The events prophesied in Revelation 11:1-13 are now far from improbable.

Who are the two witnesses? Do we know them from elsewhere in Scripture?

> These are the two olive trees and the two lamps in attendance on the Lord of the world.
> - Revelation 11:4

This is a reference to the persons mentioned in a conversation with an angel recorded in the Book of Zechariah. Zechariah saw a golden lamp stand holding seven lamps, with two olive trees beside it.

> The angel ... gave me this answer: 'These seven are the eyes of Yahweh which range over the whole world.' ... the two olive trees ... 'are the two anointed ones in attendance on the Lord of the whole world.'
> - Zechariah 4:5-14

So there are two anointed ones in attendance on the Lord, and these are the two witnesses in Revelation 11.

At other critical points in Scripture, two anointed men are present. They were present at Our Lord's Ascension into heaven forty days after his Resurrection.

> They were still staring into the sky as he went, when suddenly two men in white were standing beside them, and they said, 'Why are you standing there looking up to heaven? This Jesus who has been taken up from you into heaven will come back in the same way as you have seen him go to heaven.'
>
> Acts 1:10,11

In Luke's account, they were present when Christ rose from the dead.

> On entering, the women could not find the body of the Lord Jesus. As they stood perplexed about this, two men in shining garments stood by them. And as they were afraid, they bowed their heads to the

The Day of the Lord Draws Closer

ground, but the two men said to them, 'Why do you seek the living among the dead? He is not here. He is risen.' — Luke 24:3-6

The text in Revelation 11 attributes to the two witnesses powers which were held by Elijah and Moses. By the words of their mouth they can bring fire to slay any who come against them (verse 5). Elijah had this ability; see 1 Kings 18:38 and 2 Kings 1:10,12.

They can lock up the sky so that it doesn't rain as long as they are prophesying (verse 6). Elijah also had the power to do this; see 1 Kings 17:1.

They can turn water into blood and strike the world with any plague as often as they wish (verse 6). Moses was given the power to do this before the liberation of God's people from Egypt, see Exodus 7-10.

When Jesus was transfigured on Mount Tabor, two men appeared 'in glory,' speaking with him about his coming death in Jerusalem, on which subject his disciples were persistently hard of hearing. The two men were Moses and Elijah (Luke 9:28-36).

So, are Moses and Elijah the two witnesses of Revelation 11? There is some evidence for the view that they are. The evidence against is that they were overpowered and killed by the beast (verse 7). God breathed life back into them after three and a half days (verse 11) and they were taken up to heaven with their enemies watching (verse 12).

Is it possible for bodies to be killed after being assumed into heaven? Would it be possible for the assumed bodies of Moses and Elijah to be killed? They only remained dead for a few days, but can an assumed body be overcome by death even temporarily? Can a glorified body come down to earth and be killed? Does that seem right? Certainly it doesn't seem right, though one could argue it the other way. God can do anything.

He can certainly cause two men, born in the normal way into the generation in which they will be prophesying, to be resurrected after death and assumed into heaven. If this is what is prophesied, then we have to conclude that they will not be Moses and Elijah, but will be operating in the spirit and power both of Moses and Elijah.

St John the Baptist went forth 'in the spirit and power of Elijah' (Luke 1:17). According to what is probably the most credible reading of the text, the two witnesses in Revelation 11 will likewise go forth in the spirit and power both of Moses and Elijah.

After the two witnesses were taken up to heaven, a number of disasters came upon the city, proving that their presence and their testimony on earth were not 'a plague' as the people of the world had thought. The plague didn't come among them when the two witnesses were present. It came among them after they were taken away.

> Immediately there was a violent earthquake, and a tenth of the city collapsed; seven thousand persons were killed in the earthquake, and the survivors, overcome with fear, could only give glory to the God of heaven.   - Revelation 11:13

That they gave glory to the God of heaven is a remarkable tribute to the power of the testimony of the two witnesses. It stands in contrast to the reaction of earth's inhabitants to the other disasters described in Revelation. After the sixth trumpet was sounded and the disasters followed, the peoples of the world did not give up their idolatries and their murders and their other sins (Revelation 9:20,21). After the angel had released the seventh bowl and the plague of hail came upon the earth, the people of the earth still would not repent; rather 'they cursed God for sending a plague of hail' (Revelation 16:21).

But when the disasters occurred after the two men exercising the powers of Moses and Elijah were taken up to heaven, the peoples of the earth 'could only give glory to the God of heaven.'

How is it that Moses and Elijah, and those operating in their spirit and power, can testify with such great effect? How is it that they can bring people to repentance where nothing else can?

Moses and Elijah were filled with zeal. They were filled in their minds and their spirits with a uniquely powerful sense that the God of Israel is the only God. They knew in their bone marrow that to turn aside even in the smallest degree to other gods is the greatest tragedy that can befall God's people. That is what gives their testimony its unique power. That is why they were able to call God's people back from idolatry several thousand years ago; and that is why the two witnesses, acting in their spirit, will be able to testify with great power even in the time of the Great Apostasy.

When the Israelites built the golden calf, Moses smashed the tablets of the Law, knowing that the core and center of the Law was being tossed aside by God's people, making a mockery of the words on the tablets of the Law. Moses understood that the whole purpose of the Law was to fix the attention of God's people on the worship of Yahweh alone, in the knowledge that he, Yahweh of Israel, is the only true and saving God.

If the people of Israel were ever to seek to observe the Law while giving their praise and worship to other gods, their very observance of the Law would be an abomination, being used to honor demons and not God. This is why Moses smashing the tablets of the Law when he learned that the people had built the golden calf.

When the people of Israel were mixing the worship of the true God of Israel with the worship of Baal, Elijah was the one who called them together on Mount Carmel and raised the challenge that rings as loud and clear today as it ever did: "How long will you go hobbling on two different legs? If Yahweh is God, follow him" (1 Kings 18:21).

There is unfailing power in the pure worship of the only true God, the God of Israel who came in the flesh in Christ. And there is unfailing power in the testimony given by those who worship with this purity. Moses and Elijah are the great biblical witnesses of this. That is why they could exercise the power of God himself, because they trusted in him alone and in no other god.

Moses and Elijah succeeded in winning God's people back. They turned Israel's allegiance back from their idols and led them to dedicate themselves afresh to the true God, Yahweh of Israel. When Moses rebuked them, and again when Elijah challenged them, the people accepted their testimony and repented.

And again, even in the times of devastation leading up to the Great Day, when all seems lost for God's people on earth, when the deceiver, the serpent, seems in control of everything, even at such a time, when two men walking in the spirit of Moses and Elijah prophesy with power among us, the peoples of the earth cannot help themselves. The truth becomes clear to them. They can only give glory to the true God of heaven and to his Christ.

REVELATION 12

This chapter is an account of the enmity, the conflict in high places between Christ and Antichrist, the most ancient enmity in existence. As in all of the Book of Revelation, the author does not relate events in time sequence.

From his eternity, as we mentioned in our Introduction, before any creature was made, God conceived a plan. This plan was most delightful to God. It was most delightful to the angels too, when he made it known to them, but not to all the angels. It was most infuriating to his most gifted angel, Lucifer.

God wanted to overcome all limitations. To an angel, a pure spirit, God can give himself in all the fullness of the angel's capacity to receive him. That is a wonderful gift, greater than we can imagine; but it contains a limitation, because a spirit can only receive to the extent of its capacity to receive spiritually. God cannot give himself to an angel in all the fullness of his own Godhead, only in all the fullness of the angel's capacity to receive him spiritually.

With God there is always more. He wanted to overcome this limitation. He wanted a creature to whom he could give himself not only in all the fullness of the creature's capacity to receive him spiritually. He wanted a creature to whom he could give himself in all the fullness of his own Godhead. He cannot do that spiritually; but he can do it bodily.

That is why God created the material universe, and created a race of embodied spirits, and became an embodied spirit himself. He created the material universe in view of Christ, to accomplish the desire in his heart from eternity, to give himself to his creature without limitation, in all the fullness of his Godhead.

> For in him (Christ) dwells all the fullness of the Godhead bodily.   - Colossians 2:9

The Incarnation of the Son of God was the boldest and the riskiest plan ever conceived, but it was so great that God determined to do it in spite of the cost to himself. The Incarnation of Christ was always at the center of God's creative intentions. Through the Eucharist, God enters among his people and gives himself to them as he could never have otherwise done.

There is a tradition that, before he created any humans, he made the plans of his heart known to the angels. Those angels who remained faithful were delighted with the plan, and were delighted at the prospect of serving in the future kingdom to be ruled over by Christ.

But Lucifer, the most gifted angel, found fault with God's plan. God is a pure spirit, he reasoned, and so are angels. Therefore angels are more like God than embodied spirits could ever be. Embodied spirits are animal and spiritual at the same time. How could God decide to take on the inferior form? If he wanted to unite himself with a creature, surely he had to unite himself with the superior form, with the pure spirit? Surely he must become an angel, and not a man?

And, even more infuriating to the proud spirit, why should angels be asked to demean themselves by serving in a kingdom of second class creatures, embodied spirits, ruled over by Christ, the Son of God taking on the nature of the second class creature?

But God had decided. He would not change his mind. The eternal word of God was spoken. It would not be retracted. 'For verily he took not on him the nature of angels; but he took on him the seed of Abraham' (Hebrews 2:16).

Lucifer's pride was inflamed. He was particularly incensed at the idea that the Son of God would take flesh through the flesh of a woman, who would therefore be exalted to the position of Mother of God, and would therefore hold authority over God himself and over all his creatures, Lucifer included. How could the highest of all creatures, Lucifer, lower himself to act in the service not only of the inferior kind of spirit, an embodied spirit, but the inferior form of an embodied spirit, a woman?

But that was God's plan. 'Are they *(the angels)* not all ministering spirits, sent to serve for the sake of those who are to inherit salvation?' (Hebrews 1:14).

God's plan provoked Lucifer, the proud spirit, to a frenzy of infuriation. He made a decision. He would fight against this plan of God with all his might. He would fight it on all fronts. He would fight it violently.

He would fight it subtly. He would fight it in heaven. He would fight it on earth. He would fight against Christ himself. He would fight against his church. He would fight against his Mother. He would fight with all his energy. He would fight with all his gifts of intellect.

"I will not serve!" The cry went like lightning around all the angel hosts, together with his offers of promotion to all those who would join his alternative kingdom. A third of them joined his rebellion.

The belief that the Incarnation of Christ was made known to the angels in heaven before the creation of the material universe, and that it was the reason for Lucifer's rebellion, is not a necessary part of the faith. We don't have to believe it. We can reject it without thereby falling into heresy. It is worth noting, however, that St Louis Marie de Montfort taught it. He taught that the reason Lucifer was so infuriated at the advance revelation of the Incarnation was the position reserved in God's plan for Mary his Mother. The thought of being asked to play second fiddle to a woman was intolerable to his pride. St Louis Marie de Montfort is a canonized saint, so this belief has to be treated as approved, though it is not required.

Chapter 12 of the Book of Revelation describes the rebellion of the Antichrist in very dramatic form. The dragon, 'the ancient serpent called the devil and Satan' (verse 9) fights relentlessly against the Incarnation and the entire kingdom of Christ on all possible fronts. He fights against the angels who remained faithful (verses 7-9). He fights against the Christ Child (verse 4). He fights against the Child's Mother (verses 4,6,13-16). He fights against Christ's people, the church (verse 17).

He swept a third of the stars of heaven down to earth. He confronted the woman 'to devour the child as soon as it was born' (verse 4). He inspired Herod to use all possible means to seek out and kill Christ when he was born at Bethlehem. But the child, 'who was to rule all the nations with a rod of iron,' was taken up to God and to his throne' (verse 5).

The life and death and Resurrection of Christ are skipped in this account in verse 5, which goes straight from the dragon's attempts to devour the Child as soon as he is born to the Child's Ascension into heaven. The main focus of Revelation 12 is on the conflict here on earth while Christ is waiting at the right side of the Father until his time comes to return. The conflict is between the dragon and the woman. It reaches its climax in the times of tribulation.

'The woman escaped into the desert, where God had prepared a place for her to be taken care of for twelve hundred and sixty days' (verse 6). In some of the revelations Mary has been making to the church in recent times, she explains what is happening here.

The dragon, the proud spirit, is very skilled in public relations. He knows how to make himself look good in the material world. He knows how to place his own people in important positions to take control of media, and politics. He has control of the 'ten horns' (verse 3), the earthly rulers who in turn control the means of communication. He knows how to get his message out. He thus makes it look like he is in total control of the whole world.

The woman, by contrast, the Mother of God, makes her home among the unimportant, those of whom the world takes no notice, those 'who keep the commandments of God and have in themselves the testimony of Jesus' (verse 17). These are the people who consecrate themselves to the woman and pray the rosary as she has many times requested. These people will be kept safe in the tribulation. They may not make a big splash in the world dominated by the dragon; they are the 'least' in the kingdom ruled over by Christ; they are the ones who he said are greater even than St John the Baptist (Matthew 11:11).

As the woman provides a safe refuge against the dragon for these people, who keep God's commandments and have in themselves the testimony of Jesus, they also provide a safe refuge for her, giving her her place in 'the desert,' which is the great mass of those who do not have important positions in the world controlled by the dragon.

The text then switches to a different timeframe altogether, though it looks as if it is relating events in time sequence. It goes straight to the ancient warfare, long before the woman was born, the warfare that arose in heaven when Lucifer rebelled against the plans of God (verses 7-9). The Archangel Michael led the forces of God in this battle, and in the power of God they cast Satan out of heaven together with the angels who had joined his rebellion (verse 9).

The positioning of this account of the rebellion of Satan and his wicked angels, in between the account of the dragon's conflict with the woman and the male Child coming before, and the account of his conflict with the woman and the church coming after, indicates, I believe, the cause of Lucifer's fall, his argument with God that got him thrown out of heaven.

It is a very good example of the thematic logic underlying the sequencing of events in the Book of Revelation. Historical time is not the sole determinant in the sequence in which St John has his visions. He has a vision of the birth of the male Child and the dragon's evil designs against that birth. He then has a vision of the original battle in heaven, the outcome of which was Satan's fall and the fall of his wicked angels. The sequencing gives us the precise reason for Satan's fall: it is his hostility to the Incarnation.

Satan's downfall was his hatred of the idea of serving in the kingdom ruled over by the incarnate Son of God, and his fury at being expected to recognize a woman as the most exalted of God's creatures, supplanting him in the position he originally held. The sequencing also gives the background to the conflict we see in the world during the tribulation, the spiritual conflict in high places.

Satan is thus the original spirit of Antichrist. He hates the Incarnation of the Son of God with a hatred that rings through the ages and warns us of the depths of evil and deception in him. We are to make no compromises with the Antichrist. We are to give no heed to his weasel words. We are to 'choose none of his ways' (Proverbs 3:31).

There follows a song of rejoicing and glory to God and to Christ, because the casting down of Satan represents their decisive victory (verses 10-12); and there is a warning, bringing the action right into the present, to those who are living on earth, because the dragon's fall to earth infuriates him all the more against us. It makes him all the more determined to rob us of the victory that is offered to us in Christ (verse 12).

The mean-mindedness of the wicked spirits is clear from this. When the rich man in Luke 16 found himself in torment in hell, he at least had the humanity to appeal to Abraham on behalf of his brothers still living on earth so that they might avoid coming to such a horrible place. Instead of doing this, Satan and his angels work might and main to drag us all into the vile stench of the world of torment in which they live. The damnation they experience makes them all the more determined to cut us off from the indescribable blessings we are offered through faith in Christ.

The plans of God are completely intolerable to the pride of the devil. Christ offers us liberation, healing, peace, joy that cannot be described, together with the gift of his very self. Satan wants to rob us of all of these things in order to add us to his horrible kingdom, to enslave us as subjects of his horrible rule.

'The serpent vomited water from his mouth like a flood after the woman, that she might be carried away by the flood' (verse 15). The water from the dragon's mouth has been interpreted by Mary, in some of her communications with the church, as the flood of talk against the doctrines of the Church. It proceeds out of the mouth of Satan and spreads throughout the world, robbing countless numbers of the most precious gift of their faith, which is the source of all their power. Faith in the only true God and in his Christ is what gives us our power against the forces of darkness.

The doctrines of the Church always establish us in our faith in Christ. The doctrine of the Incarnation necessarily looms large in this, and because Mary was God's chosen instrument in bringing about the Incarnation, the doctrines concerning Mary are indispensible to our understanding of who Christ is. Small wonder therefore that in disgorging his flood of high sounding nonsense against true doctrine, the dragon takes aim against Mary.

The flood of water from the dragon's mouth is designed to rob us of our faith, and so to rob us of our power to resist him and his wicked angels. It is designed to attack our faith at its very roots. A leading freemason once famously said, 'get them to question the dogmas and they are already masons without the apron.'

Yes, Satan wants to rob us of the dogmas, because they are the foundations of our strength. At the center of our faith is the Incarnation, and because the Incarnation took effect through the Mother of God, the river of filth vomited out of the dragon's mouth is directed against Mary.

'But the earth came to her rescue; it opened its mouth and swallowed the flood spewed from the dragon's mouth' (verse 16). The ten horns under the dragon's control keep spewing a flood of words to throw people into confusion. The important persons of the world give heed to the flood of words and so lose the protection and the blessings of their most holy and precious faith. But again the earth, the desert, the great mass of the unimportant who cling to the commandments of God and the testimony of Jesus, who heed Mary's warnings and keep themselves under her protection, these give Mary safe sanctuary, as she gives safe sanctuary to them, and against them the flood of diabolical words is thus rendered harmless.

These are the people who ignore the words of Satan and his ten horns and give their attention instead to the everlasting word of God, the doctrines of the faith long established in the Church, the counsels of Mary and her invitations to prayer, especially the rosary.

'Then the dragon was enraged with the woman, and went away to make war on the rest of her children, who obey the commandments of God, and have in themselves the testimony of Jesus' (verse 17). This verse makes it clear beyond doubt that those who keep God's commandments and have in themselves the testimony of Jesus are the children of Mary and the arch enemies of the dragon.

The Incarnation is the key to the test of spirits given by the apostle John. We know whether we are dealing with good spirits or wicked spirits by applying this test:

> Every spirit that confesses Jesus Christ come in the flesh is of God; and every spirit that does not confess Jesus Christ come in the flesh is not of God but is of that spirit of Antichrist whose coming you have heard of. He is already at large in the world.
>
> - 1 John 4:2,3

We must never lose sight of this test, this distinction between the good spirits and the wicked spirits. 'Hereby know we the spirit of truth, and the spirit of error' (1 John 4:6). The spirit of truth is in love with the Incarnation of Christ. The spirit of error is implacably hostile to it.

This is why we have so many indications in Scripture that the Day of the Lord will be preceded by the abolition of the Eucharist and the placing of the abomination of desolation where it ought not to be. The spirit of Antichrist will do everything in his power to destroy the Eucharist, because the Eucharist is the fulfillment of the deepest desire of God's heart, the desire that led him to think of Christ and of the created universe: his desire to give himself to his creature without limitation, not restricted to the creature's limited capacity to receive him spiritually, but to give himself in all the fullness of his own Godhead, bodily.

Chapter 12 of the Book of Revelation makes one thing totally clear: If we want to belong to Christ and take our place in his kingdom, we must honor our baptismal vows; we must utterly reject Satan and all his works, and all his empty promises. There can be no compromise. The devil was a liar from the beginning. He is the father of lies (John 8:44). And his original lie, the lie that begets all other lies, is his denial of Christ, his furious rejection of the Incarnation.

Keep a clear mind on this, adhere to Christ and his church, utterly reject the father of lies and all his words and all his works, and all his empty promises, and you have received the whole message of Scripture.

In the end times struggle that has already come upon us, there is need for special protection, because the devil, knowing that his time is short, has come down on us with a wrath that threatens to overpower us. God has given us a safe refuge in the storm. We can have recourse to Mary as a most powerful means to stay strong in faith and true to his word without any fear of being on the wrong side of Scripture as some Christians believe.

Our scriptural assurance on this point is in this twelfth chapter of the Book of Revelation. We can be very confident about this because Mary is at the very heart of the argument. The spirit of Antichrist is at war with the Incarnation. The Incarnation was brought about through Mary, who is therefore at the center of the warfare against the dragon. She is not destined to lose in that warfare.

Does it appear in Revelation 12 that Mary is vulnerable in her conflict with the dragon? The dragon is portrayed as coming against her very aggressively; Mary is portrayed as needing to escape from his attacks.

If Mary is portrayed as vulnerable in the face of Satan, this would seem to be at odds with what we know of the power she exercises over the devil and all his hordes of followers. She has total coercive power over all demons, including Satan. She is given this power by God. Exorcists are well aware of this. They will tell you that as soon as Mary arrives on the scene the game is up for the demons. As soon as Mary shows up, the demons are already gone.

Is this contradicted in Revelation 12 when it seems to portray Mary as vulnerable?

Mary is greatly grieved at the numbers of souls lost to the enemy. In that sense she can be said to be vulnerable. However, her own total coercive power over demons is not affected by this. Anyone whomsoever who appeals to Mary for help is already delivered from demons. Her power over them, given to her by Almighty God, is absolute. Don't forget the details of the great sign in heaven at the beginning of the chapter:

> A great sign appeared in heaven: a woman clothed with the sun, with the moon under her feet, and upon her head a crown of twelve stars.
>
> - Revelation 12:1

This is a description of a person with royal power. The moon is 'under her feet.' The crescent moon has always been the symbol of pagan religion, religion that cannot and will not accept the kingship and Divinity of Jesus, religion under the authority of Satan, the dragon, the Antichrist. In the image of Our Lady of Guadalupe in Mexico City, the crescent moon is under her feet with the two edges pointed outward and upward, like the horns of a dragon.

It is worth remembering that a well attested tradition, with full Church approval, tells us that the image of Our Lady of Guadalupe in Mexico City was placed on a shepherd's cloak by Mary herself. To my knowledge it is the only publicly venerated image of Our Lady which was made by Our Lady herself. That this image shows her with the crescent moon under her feet is as completely appropriate as it is completely biblical.

The symbolism of the crescent moon existed in the time of the Judges of Israel, about 1200 b.c., and no doubt much earlier.

> Then Gideon arose and slew Zebah and Zalmunnah; and took away the crescents from their camels' necks.   - Judges 8:21

It was permitted to take the spoils of war, so Gideon was allowed to take possession of the camels. It was not permitted to take any idolatrous objects as part of the booty (see Deuteronomy 7:25,26), so he had to remove the crescent moons from their necks before taking the camels.

The woman of Revelation 12 has the crescent moon under her feet. There is no question about the absolute authority given to her by God over the entire kingdom of evil.

REVELATION 13

The dragon went away to make war on those who keep the commandments of God and have in themselves the testimony of Jesus. He has made war with the hosts of heaven, and got thrown out. He has sought to devour the infant Jesus as soon as he was born, and was frustrated in that. He has sought to overcome the woman, the Mother of God, and failed in that too. His warfare against the church now begins.

Chapter 13 gives an account of mass movements rising up among the peoples of the world in opposition to Christ and his church. These mass movements are all the work of the ancient dragon, the spirit of Antichrist, Satan with his wicked angels. The mass movements are interconnected.

> And I stood on the shore of the sea, and saw a beast rise up out of the sea, having seven heads, and ten horns, and upon his horns ten crowns, and upon his heads were names of blasphemy.   - Revelation 13:1

The sea here symbolizes all of humanity living on the earth. Now, in his vision, St John sees a movement rising up among the nations of the earth. He calls this movement a beast. The heads and the horns of the beast symbolize the rulers of nations and the power they hold over the means of communication.

The beast cannot be ignored, because he has power over nations and over what people are allowed to hear and to see and to read in the means of communication. Blasphemy, the perversion of the knowledge of God, the attempt to rob God's people of the priceless gift of the faith, are at the center of the beast's purposes.

The seven heads and ten horns of the beast reflect the seven heads and ten horns of the red dragon in Revelation 12:3. This seems to mean either that the empire of each among the nations of the earth is coextensive, or that the empire of the beast parallels the dragon's empire in 'the heavens,' the high places of spiritual wickedness, where Satan rules over the wicked angels who joined in his rebellion against God and the plans of God in Christ.

> And the beast which I saw was like a leopard, and his feet were the feet of a bear, and his mouth as the mouth of a lion; and the dragon gave him his power, and his throne, and his immense authority.
>
> - Revelation 13:2

This begins the characterization of the first beast. He is compared to wild and dangerous animals. The dragon delegates all his own power and authority to this beast.

> I saw that one of his heads seemed to have had a fatal injury, and this deadly wound was healed, and all the world marveled and followed the beast. They prostrated themselves in front of the dragon because he had given his authority to the beast, and they prostrated themselves in front of the beast, saying, 'Who is like the beast? Who is able to make war with him?'
>
> - Revelation 13:3,4

How should we interpret verse 3, about the beast's fatal wound which was healed? The fatal wound which was healed points in general to reversions to paganism after

Christianity has been established in a place. We see this happening across much of the world as I write this. As once Christian nations lose the true faith and turn to sinful practices, their spiritual hunger remains, and feeds on the demonic, on the pagan. The head of the antichristian beast, long overpowered by the Light of Christ, begins to come back to horrible life.

The resurgence of paganism in postchristian settings is a much greater evil, a much more deliberate sin with much more serious consequences, because it involves the rejection of Christ by those who have already come to know his blessings.

The rejection of Christ helps to explain the 'blasphemous titles' on the heads of the beast. The whole world marveled and followed the beast. They prostrated themselves before the dragon, and they prostrated themselves before the beast.

The beast's purpose, specified in verse 4, is to lead all the peoples of the world into false worship, to tear the allegiance of God's holy people away from Christ and to win it for the dragon and for the beast himself. He wants all the peoples of the world to give to him the dedication of themselves they should be giving to the true God, the God who took flesh in Christ.

The rise of Islam in the countries of the Middle East and North Africa, the countries which denoted the larger world in biblical writing, was a pushback against the spread of Christianity, which had sunk deep roots in these countries. Islam rejects the doctrine of Christ as the Son of God; and as Jesus said, you cannot reject Christ and still have God. 'He who rejects me rejects the one who sent me' (Luke 10:16).

And the peoples of the world capitulate. 'Who is like the beast?' These words mirror the words contained in the name of St Michael the archangel, who led the warfare in heaven against Lucifer with the cry, 'Who is like God?' We can see in this text that the dragon begins to succeed in his evil purpose, to induce people to stop worshiping Christ and to worship Antichrist instead.

The peoples of the world give up. They fall for the beast's lie. They believe he is invincible. 'Who is able to make war with him?' Weak in faith, they decide that the fight is futile. By their timidity they grant the beast the victories he needs in order to rule over them.

> There was given to the beast a mouth speaking boasts and blasphemies, and power was given to him to continue for forty two months. And he opened his mouth in blasphemy against God, to blaspheme his name, and his tabernacle, and those who dwell in heaven. And it was given to him to make war with the saints and to overcome them, and power was given to him over all races, and peoples, and languages, and nations. And all that dwell upon the earth will worship him, whose names are not written since the foundation of the world in the book of life of the Lamb who was slain.   - Revelation 13:5-8

'And his tabernacle.' This is an explicit reference, rare in the Book of Revelation, to the Eucharist as the focus of the dragon's attack against the church.

The prophecies in this passage have been fulfilled already, at least in part, in the rise of Islam among the once Christian countries of the Middle East, and much later in the rise of Communism in the 1900s. The arrogant tyrants who have risen up and made war against nations to build up their own empires, have invariably been blasphemers against God and persecutors of his church.

Freemasonry, which is closely linked with Islam through its symbols and rituals, promotes both these and other blasphemies. The secret brotherhoods in general, which are syncretistic and fundamentally antichristian, of Freemasonry and its offshoots in Shrinerism and other organizations, have a long tradition of taking Islamic symbols as part of their paraphernalia. Some of them have the practice of wearing the Fez hat, symbolizing 'victory' over the Christian martyrs. Some of them take Mecca and other centers of Islam as points of reference in their rituals.

The spiritual linkage between Islam and these groups has to do, I believe, with the harlot of Babylon and the scarlet beast she rides. We will discuss this later in speaking of Revelation 17 and 18.

The text then turns to a second beast, sharing the same purpose and the same authority as the first beast and acting on the first beast's behalf.

> And I saw a second beast emerging from the ground; he had two horns like a lamb, and he spoke like a dragon. And he exercised all the power of the first beast, and caused all the earth and those who dwell therein to worship the first beast, whose deadly wound had healed. - Revelation 13:11,12

This second beast induces the peoples of the world to worship the first beast; but his appearance is much milder. The beast like a lamb looks much less menacing than the beast like a leopard.

The beast like a lamb is the false prophet, who will claim authority over the Church for three and a half years leading up to the Day of the Lord. He is the man of iniquity prophesied by Daniel and by St Paul in 2 Thessalonians 2:1-12.

The beast like a lamb is also a reference to the Christians who fall away from true faith and entangle themselves in freemasonry. The man of iniquity will need to take false power over the church, and to do this he will need to have the assistance of Christians operating in the shadowy world of masonry with its control over media and information flows.

These apostate Christians, together with the false prophet, make up the second beast, the beast that looks like a lamb.

I am very conscious of the risks entailed in this reading of the text about the second beast. Even now, in some fringe discussions, there are crazy claims going around that the man of iniquity is already seated on the Chair of Peter. The events prophesied in the above text are probably centuries in the future, and in any event, we must always keep the words of Our Lord in mind: "He who hears you hears me, and he who rejects you rejects me, and he who rejects me rejects the one who sent me" (Luke 10:16).

Reverence for the Church, for her sacraments, for her pastors, is an integral part of our faith. If we allow ourselves to be deceived into becoming hostile to the Church and her pastors, we lose the grace of God and we become powerless against the attacks of our spiritual enemies.

Even if a minority of pastors fall short and need to be corrected, we must not turn against them. We must pray and, if we can do it, act for their rehabilitation. We must never use the faults of a few to turn against the pastors of the Church in general. Never forget what we owe to our pastors. 'Remember your leaders who preached the word of God to you' (Hebrews 13:7).

And never forget that when we let the Church down, the Church doesn't walk away from us. Neither, if the Church ever lets us down, should we walk away from the Church.

Remember too that the time of the Church's crisis leading up to the Day of the Lord, when the daily sacrifice will be abolished for three and a half years and the abomination of desolation put in its place, will only serve to prove how inexpressibly holy the Church is. In mobilizing all his armies against the Church and her ministers, our enemy the devil targets the Eucharist to pervert it into a false offering to the glory of himself. There can be only one reason he targets the Eucharist like this: he knows it is at the center of God's plan to bless us. If he could topple the Church which makes the Eucharist possible, he would succeed in robbing us of all our blessings.

He will throw everything he has into his attempt to topple the Church, but he will fail. We have the promise from the lips of Our Lord that the gates of hell will not prevail against the Church (Matthew 16:18).

The false prophet referred to in Revelation 13:11-18 is also referred to in Revelation 16:13, 19:20 and 20:10. He works in intimate cooperation with the beast and he shares his fate, being thrown with the beast into the lake of fire at the end of the warfare on the Day of the Lord.

> And he worked great miracles, even calling fire down from heaven to earth in the sight of men. And he deceived those who dwell on the earth by means of those miracles which he had power to do in the sight of the beast; saying to those who dwell on the earth that they should make an image to the beast, who had the wound by a sword, and yet lived. And

he had power to give life to the image of the beast, that the image of the beast should both speak and have everyone who refused to worship the image of the beast put to death. - Revelation 13:13-15

This is the only passage in the New Testament, at least that I know of, which provides detail of how the abomination of desolation will take place. Preternatural (demonic) power at work in the man of iniquity will bring about wonders which will induce great numbers of people to fall in behind the beast's leadership.

The deception will gather pace until a statue is erected honoring devils. The penalty for failure to worship the statue will be death.

And he caused all, both small and great, rich and poor, slave and citizen, to receive a mark on their right hand, or on their foreheads: that no one might buy or sell, unless he had the mark, or the name of the beast, or the number of his name.
- Revelation 13:16,17

The beast like a lamb will take authority over the world's financial and trading systems. Only those who come into line with his evil agenda will be able to benefit. This all has a familiar ring to it in the age we live in. It doesn't take an exceptional imagination to foresee this prophecy coming to pass.

The branding on the right hand or forehead looks like a counter move against the same practice among God's people to remind them of their liberation from slavery and their consecration as God's holy people. See Exodus 13:9,16, Deuteronomy 6:8 and the seals of God written on the foreheads of God's people in Revelation 7:3, 9:4, 14:1, and 22:4. See also Ezekiel 9:4-6 and the crosses written by the angel on the foreheads of all those in Jerusalem who had taken no part in the idolatries then being committed in the Temple.

See also the name written on the forehead of the harlot of Babylon in Revelation 17:5 – 'Mystery of Babylon the Great, Mother of Harlots and Abominations of the Earth.'

There is a practice in Islam of wearing Islamic symbols on armbands and headbands. No doubt there will be further instances of marks on hands and foreheads with the growing domination of Antichrist leading up to the enthronement of the man of iniquity, the abolition of the daily sacrifice, the installation of the abomination of desolation in its place, and the terrifying clean up that will then take place on the Day of the Lord.

The prohibition against buying and selling looks like something that could be enforced by the surveillance state, this sinister thing we see developing in our present world. In future centuries it will probably be easy for sinister powers to enforce such a prohibition through the payment mechanism and the growing intrusion of information technology into people's lives. Recent developments in information technology have made these prophecies wholly credible, where they might have looked fanciful only a few decades ago.

> This calls for wisdom: Let him who has understanding interpret the number of the beast: for it is the number of a man; his number is six hundred and sixty six. - Revelation 13:18

Many attempts at explaining this verse have been made and it is sometimes difficult to know how seriously to take them. The Antichrist, or Satan, always tries to pass himself off as being greater than God, greater than Christ. 'I will rival the Most High,' Lucifer boasts in Isaiah 14:14. Interpretations that reflect this ludicrous claim of superiority over God will usually have something to recommend them.

The most intriguing explanation I've heard is offered by Walid Shoebat, who noticed a similarity between the Greek characters for 666 and the Arabic characters for the name Islam. His theory is that the apostle John, in his vision, saw the Greek characters as he was writing in Greek, had no knowledge of the Arabic characters and in any event Islam did not exist at the time he was writing. He naturally wrote down the Greek characters for 666, unwittingly identifying the name of the beast for future generations as Islam.

If this theory is true, then the prophecy of 666 refers to something that could not have been understood by any human being, not even the human biblical author, at the time it was written down.

Does the Holy Spirit give information to the human biblical author which the author himself cannot understand, but which is to be understood at a later time in salvation history?

It sounds a little far fetched. And yet there are examples in Scripture of texts which could not have been understood by their human author, but which became comprehensible later with the coming of Our Lord. One example of this is the Jacob's ladder text in Genesis 28:12. Jacob dreamed of a ladder reaching up to heaven on which the angels of God were going up and coming down, and the dream filled him with mysterious joy.

This only became comprehensible when Jesus said to Nathanael: "Truly, truly I tell you, you will see heaven opened and the angels of God ascending and descending upon the Son of Man" (John 1:52). Another example is the bronze serpent of Numbers 21:9, which only became comprehensible when Jesus compared it with his own lifting up on the Cross in John 3:14.

'It is the number of a man' (Revelation 13:18). Can Shoebat explain how a number representing an entire religion can be the number of a man? He can. The word 'number,' in his reading, is better rendered as 'multitude,' being the multitude of the man's followers rather than the number representing the man himself. Hence the number refers to the religion as the totality of its members, all following a single founder.

I can't comment authoritatively on this theory as I know neither Greek nor Arabic. I mention it in passing because I think that of all the interpretations of 666 that I've come across, it at least has the appearance of having a real foundation.

What makes it hard to accept is that it is based on an alleged mistake on the part of the human biblical author. It amounts to an assertion that the Holy Spirit showed St John an expression in one language which St John interpreted in another language. There are no other examples of this in Scripture, so far as I know, and I cannot help feeling that it runs counter to the principle enunciated by St Paul: 'For God is not the author of confusion' (1 Corinthians 14:33).

The theory therefore has to be taken with something of a pinch of salt, but if it were to be found true, then it would mean that the Bible has condemned Islam by name. It has already condemned the teaching of Islam that God does not have a Son (in 1 John 2:22-24 for example). If the Greek characters for 666 are very similar to the Arabic characters for Islam, and if the Holy Spirit had the Arabic characters in mind in giving John his vision, then we have an explicit declaration in Scripture that the beast is identified with Islam.

By extension, the beast would also have to be identified with the movements aligned to Islam against Christ and his church. Freemasonry and Shrinerism, and related brotherhoods, would have to be included.

In any event, whether Shoebat's theory is true or not, these movements all appear to be described in Revelation 13.

We keep in mind also that the spirit of Antichrist is at work in all movements which are hostile to Christ and his church. We recognize the activity of the devil in all such movements. Don't forget that when the dragon is introduced in Revelation 12:3 he is referred to as 'a huge red dragon.' It is hardly an accident that atheistic Marxism, one of the most murderous outbreaks of Antichrist in history, actually calls itself by the same name, the Red Dragon.

Both atheistic Marxism and Islam have been openly and violently hostile toward Christ and his church. The beast like a leopard, Freemasonry, has adopted more subtle tactics against the church. It does not declare its hand. Secrecy is its oxygen. It acts effectively to promote sinister ideas in place of God's word and his commandments, and to this end takes control of the means of communication in the world.

The Book of Revelation makes it clear that this beast of Freemasonry is intimately aligned with the more violent forms of Antichrist, and its essential violence will come into the open as the climax approaches leading up to the Day of the Lord.

That climax will last for a short time only, and will be quickly followed by the definitive victory of Christ and his effective kingship in all the nations of the earth. But it will happen, and while it happens the time will not seem short. Three and a half years can look like eternity when horrific things are happening. The mystery of iniquity will break out in events so horrible they are hard to contemplate. Great numbers will be deceived by the apostasy, from every nation on earth, before Christ intervenes to bring about the terrifying remedy.

But those who have placed themselves under the protection of the woman will not be deceived. Those who pray her rosary, and keep God's commandments, and have in themselves the testimony of Jesus, will receive protection so powerful that they will not be part of the general falling away. To know Mary is to know who Christ is. To know Mary is to know the Incarnation. To know Mary is to be powerfully protected from error and confusion.

If you remain close to Mary, you cannot be deceived as to who the true and living God is, the one who took flesh in Christ. The dragon has no way through to those who live in the presence of Mary. For this reason, in reading the Book of Revelation we need to read Chapter 12 alongside Chapter 13, because we need to know who is leading in the warfare against the dragon, and under whose patronage we will see victory.

Christ has been taken up to heaven; he is still present and active with us, of course; but for his own good reasons, he has placed Mary at the head of the warfare here on earth during the latter times. We know this from Revelation 12. We need to know it if we are to escape the dragon's deceptions.

The very expression 'Mother of God' contains all those very truths of faith which it is the dragon's aim to steal from us. The repeated call to Mary as the 'Mother of God' strikes against the head of the enemy with all the force of a piledriver, exposing the wicked plans of the devil and his angels and sending them running for cover. The repeated call to Mary as the 'Mother of God' therefore forms an invincible wall of protection around us, making it impossible for those who recite the rosary to fall into error.

As Scripture prophetically shows Mary saying, 'I was a wall ... then was I in his presence as one who finds true peace' (Song of Songs 8:10). Mary is a wall. The wall is formed by her unfailing allegiance to the only living and true God and her unrelenting rejection of all those filthy spirits who dare to raise themselves aloft to rival him for our allegiance.

That is why Mary repels demonic deception far more quickly than the sun drives away the darkness of night. She invites all of us to take refuge behind the wall she forms against her enemies and ours.

REVELATION 17 AND 18

The seven trumpets have been blown. The seven plagues have been emptied from the seven bowls by the seven angels. The Day of the Lord is at last at hand.

In Chapters 17 and 18 we have an account of the harlot of Babylon and of the fall of the city.

A question arises, whether the fall of Babylon comes before the Day of the Lord, or whether it is a description of events taking place on that Day. The passage in Isaiah 34:5-11, which recounts the same events, indicates that it is part of the Day of the Lord. 'For this is the Day of the Lord's vengeance, the year of retribution for the controversy of Zion' (Isaiah 34:8).

The prophecy in Revelation 17 is unusual in that a detailed key is provided explaining all its symbols. The harlot is described in a set of symbols in verses 1-7. The interpretation of each symbol is then given in verses 8-18.

The harlot 'is enthroned beside many waters' (Revelation 17:1). The waters in question are explained in verse 15: 'The waters you saw, beside which the harlot is sitting, are all the peoples, and multitudes, and nations and languages.'

Who is the harlot? 'The woman you saw is the great city which has authority over all the rulers on earth' (verse 18).

Where is this city? The angel 'took me in spirit to a desert, and there I saw a woman riding a scarlet beast …' (verse 3). So the scene described is set in the desert. Is this the desert of Arabia? Yes, I believe it is. This is confirmed in Isaiah 34, which describes the destruction as taking place in 'Bozrah' and 'Edom' (Isaiah 34:6) which are in western Arabia and were shorthand for Arabia in the language of the Israelites.

The description of the scarlet beast upon which the woman is riding matches the description of the beast in Revelation 13. Compare the descriptions:

> Then I saw a beast emerging from the sea: it had seven heads and ten horns, and its heads were marked with blasphemous titles.
>
> - Revelation 13:1-3

> I saw a woman riding a scarlet beast which had seven heads and ten horns and had blasphemous titles written all over it.   - Revelation 17:3-8

We mentioned earlier that this beast is a worldwide affinity between the religion of Islam and the secret brotherhoods of Masonry, Shrinerism and related groups.

The angel further explains the identity of the beast by reference to the peoples and kingdoms of the earth:

> 'The seven heads are seven hills, on which the woman is sitting. The seven heads are also seven emperors ... the ten horns which you saw are ten kings ... They are all of one mind in putting their strength and their powers at the beast's disposal, and they will go to war against the Lamb; but because the Lamb is Lord of lords and King of kings, he will defeat them, he and his followers, the called, the chosen, the trustworthy.'   - Revelation 17:9-14

Hills, or mountains, in biblical prophetic language, refer to the nations and empires of the earth. This is why the seven heads symbolize seven hills as well as seven emperors; the two terms are not contradictory.

The angel goes on to say that the ten horns and the beast will turn against the harlot and will destroy her. She will not be destroyed by direct warfare against the Lamb and his forces; she will be destroyed by division within the enemy camp. The city in the desert of Arabia will be destroyed by the other kingdoms of the earth.

Can we match this with what we see in the world of our time? Do we see forces building up toward the climax described in the following chapter, Revelation 18, of the complete destruction of Babylon together with the wealth and luxury she brought to the peoples of the earth?

The harlot is the one 'with whom the kings of the earth have committed fornication, and the inhabitants of the earth have been made drunk with the wine of her fornication ... and upon her forehead was the name written, Mystery, Babylon the Great, the Mother of Harlots and Abominations of the Earth' (17:2-5).

The woman was also 'drunk with the blood of the saints, and the blood of the martyrs of Jesus' (17:6).

If we can identify the nature of the fornication of the harlot with the rulers of the earth, we will have all the clues we need to understand these two chapters of Revelation.

There is more in question here than the religion which has long prevailed throughout the Middle East and North Africa, the religion of Islam. We can identify the woman with Mecca, the city of pilgrimage in Arabia, 'the desert,' where people converge from all over the world to venerate the very ancient black stone, and circle in great numbers around the building housing it.

No doubt Mecca and the black stone are at the center of the account, but I think there is more to it than that. The people who come from all over the earth on pilgrimage to Mecca, and move in circles around the black stone, are all Muslims; but the harlot is fornicating with all the kings of the earth, not only with those of a single religion.

We know that fornication in biblical language refers to spiritual fornication, the turning of God's people to the veneration of idols and to a syncretism which lines up idols alongside the true God. The true God utterly abominates this syncretism.

The harlot is riding the beast with the seven heads and the ten horns. There is a relationship of interdependence between the harlot and all the kingdoms and empires of the world. What is this relationship?

We know that the beast belongs to the spirit of Antichrist. We know that the secret brotherhoods controlling the media throughout the world espouse syncretistic religion and are happy to align themselves with Islamic names and symbols for the corruption of the faith of Christians. We know that they control the media for this end too.

The fornication between the harlot and the rulers of the earth and its peoples is a spiritual fornication. Its effect is to make war on the faith of Christians, to turn them toward idols, and to destroy the purity of their faith. Islam has done this by force of arms. Masonry does it by more subtle but no less effective means.

The connecting material in the fornication, at least in the world we have seen up to now, is oil. Please don't misunderstand me. I am not making the case against the use of fossil fuels for energy. I am not suggesting that it is immoral to work in the oil business.

I am only pointing out that the nature of the interdependence between the western powers and the harlot of Babylon is economic. That is the reason for the mourning of the merchants of the earth described in Revelation 18 when they see Babylon going up in smoke. The destruction of the oilfields of Arabia, and no doubt oilfields elsewhere as well, will bring down the commercial and financial systems of the world on an unthinkable scale.

How does oil 'fuel' the spiritual fornication between the harlot and the peoples of the earth? The use of oil throughout the world as an essential energy source in industry and transport provides the rulers of the oil rich countries with all the financial power they need to preserve antichristian religion intact, and to drive out the churches of the Lamb from their territories.

The place of oil in the industrial systems of the rest of the world helps the Masonic and other brotherhoods we have spoken of to maintain the mutual influence between them and the rulers of the oil rich countries, as well as to hold control of the communications media and use it to corrupt the faith of Christians.

The objective of the fornication is shared by both parties to it, the harlot of Babylon and the rulers of the kingdoms of the earth. The objective is to wipe out the Christian faith in all the nations of the earth, and to replace it with the worship of false gods.

One of the things that at the present time make this all the easier to credit is the succession of events in recent decades known as 'the Arab Spring.' In the year 2002 the countries of the Middle East and North Africa were ruled by relatively western friendly leaders who tolerated the Christian churches then existing in their territories, though they were not willing to allow them to grow. Radical Islamic groups disliked these rulers, and began plotting to bring them down and replace them with rulers who would enforce Islam more violently and would drive any remaining Christianity from their midst.

They largely succeeded in their aim. In Iraq, in Egypt, in Tunisia, in Libya, the western friendly rulers were toppled and replaced with regimes more to the liking of the radical Islamists. They have been trying to do the same in Syria, but the resistance there has been stronger.

What is truly mystifying is that the western powers, rather than coming to the defence of their allies the western friendly rulers, actually participated decisively in bringing them down. They actually shared the aim of the radical Antichristian elements seeking the regime changes, and at decisive points they even intervened to help them.

The western media dressed up and presented the movement of radicalization as a thirst for 'democracy' among younger Muslims and gave it the title, 'the Arab Spring.' In this way they used their power over public opinion through their control of the media to make their support for radicals look praiseworthy.

The effect of the military assistance given by the western powers to radical Islamists has been to create chaos across large sections of the Middle East and North Africa, to wipe out ancient Christian communities in the process, and to extend the influence of antichristian religion in western countries.

Why did the western powers do this? Why did they consider it in their interests? Were they seeking to profit from sales of arms, acting treacherously against those leaders who had allied with them? Maybe, but I don't believe it was as simple as that. There was an underlying spiritual motivation. In fact I would regard that whole movement as totally incomprehensible if I did not have the benefit of Revelation 17 and 18, pointing to the link between western Freemasonry and radical Islam by way of the spiritual fornication taking effect through the oil trade.

The powers at work behind the scenes in the west have the same aim as do the powers at work in Islam: They both aim at the destruction of the church. Once we understand this, the details in Chapters 17 and 18 of Revelation all fall into place.

It will all come to an end in the time of the Day of the Lord. When, in the account at the end of Revelation 11, the Seventh angel sounds his trumpet, voices in heaven are heard giving glory to God and announcing the arrival of his Day. Their proclamation ends with these words:

> 'The time has come to destroy those who are destroying the earth.'   - Revelation 11:18

Is this a hint that the Bible takes a side in the environmentalist argument? Are those who are destroying the earth doing so by the excessive use of fossil fuels? It is not an issue I wish to take up in this work, but I think it worth mentioning as a possible reading of this verse, with an intriguing read-across to Revelation 17 and 18.

The destruction is designed by God to bear a spiritual fruit: the people of God are called to come out from the harlot, to convert from all false and syncretistic religion and to give their allegiance only to the God and Father of Our Lord Jesus Christ (Revelation 18:4).

Those who became super rich by the harlot of Babylon will be in mourning. They will stand at a safe distance and bewail her destruction as the smoke of her burning ascends to heaven. This use of earthy language indicates that we are not only speaking of symbols. The oil fields really will go up in smoke.

> And the kings of the earth, who have committed fornication and held orgies with her, shall bewail her and lament for her, when they shall see the smoke of her burning, standing afar off for the fear of her torment. They will say: 'Mourn, mourn for that great city, Babylon, that mighty city; in one short hour your doom has come upon you.'
>
> - Revelation 18:9,10

Recall Isaiah 34, where 'the smoke of her burning' is referred to. It takes place in Bozrah and Edom (Arabia) during 'the Day of the Lord's vengeance, the year of recompense for the controversy of Zion. Its streams will turn to pitch, its dust into brimstone, its country will turn into blazing pitch' (Isaiah 34:9).

At the end of Revelation 18, however, we are reminded to shed no tears over the harlot's passing. We are not to join with the business moguls in bewailing the loss of her. The harlot has meant nothing for God's people except destruction.

> In her was found all the blood of prophets and saints, and all the blood that was ever shed on earth.
>
> - Revelation 18:24

'And all the blood that was ever shed on earth.' There is a whole world of significance in these words. We are looking here at the work of a spirit of death who has been active throughout history. The spirit at work in the harlot of Babylon is the devil, the Antichrist. "He was a murderer from the beginning," Jesus tells us (John 8:44). He brought death into our world through the temptation and Original Sin of our first parents.

That is why the destruction of the harlot of Babylon, the destruction of the oil fields and the oil industry, the defeat of the peoples coming against Israel and against the church – these are all part of the warfare which will take place on the Great and Terrible Day of the Lord. He will win complete victory on that Day.

Revelation 17 and 18 set out in some detail the manner in which the financial and trading systems of the world are linked with spiritual fornication in the run up to the Day of the Lord. They are an example of this process which is referred to throughout Scripture. Israel was continuously turning to idolatry and to syncretistic religious practice because of the pressure brought on business people to swear by the gods of their more economically powerful neighbors.

The peoples of the modern world have similarly had their minds confused by the necessity to work and do their business in a world dominated by syncretistic thought and practice, a world of work and business in which it becomes practically impossible to confess Christ with a clear voice for fear of treading on the supposed 'sensitivities' of those who walk in the spirit of Antichrist.

What these two chapters of Revelation tell us is that the Day of the Lord will resolve this problem once and for all, in Israel, in the church, and throughout the world. The victory gained by the Lord on that Day will enable the peoples and nations of the entire world, because they will be subject to Christ, to trade with each other under the blessing of Christ. His name will be one, he will have rid the earth of the spirit of impurity, and he will have locked up the dragon in the Abyss of hell where he will be held for a thousand years, restrained from troubling God's people during all that time.

REVELATION 19 AND 20

The Rider in Revelation 19:11-21 is the Messiah, the Christ, for whom heaven opens as he marches out at the head of his armies to fight the beast, and the rulers on earth and their armies all gathered around the beast.

Each detail of the Rider signifies that he is Our Divine Lord. 'His eyes were flames of fire' (19:12, see Revelation 1:14). 'His name is, The Word of God' (19:13, see John 1:1). He is the King of kings and Lord of lords (19:16). 'From his mouth came a sharp sword' (19:15, see Revelation 1:16). 'His cloak was soaked in blood' (19:13, see Isaiah 63:1-4).

The emphasis on the divinity of the Rider, his invulnerability, his command over the armies of heaven, might make it appear that he is different from the Warrior Messiah of other prophecies. We do not have the more intimate descriptions of rays of power flashing from his hands as in Habakkuk 3:4; we do not see, at least in this passage, the Israelites' sudden and deeply affective recognition of their Messiah, as they look on the one whom they have pierced and mourn for him as for an only son, following an outpouring of grace and prayer from the Lord (Zechariah 12:10).

Once we examine the details, however, we see easily that the description of the Rider in Revelation 19:11-21 is far from being at odds with the earlier descriptions of the Day of the Lord. On the contrary, the description matches the earlier prophecies at every point, and the details of the warfare make it clear that it is the same warfare. We can pick out the links point by point:

1. The Warrior Messiah is also called the Rider in Deuteronomy 33:26, Psalm 45:4 and Psalm 68:33.
2. 'His eyes were flames of fire' (verse 12) – this is similar to the detail in Ezekiel 38:18 of his 'fury coming up in his face.' It is powerful confirmation that Ezekiel was speaking of a visible intervention of Christ in his humanity.
3. 'His cloak was soaked in blood' (verse 13) – this is the same information as in Isaiah 63:1-3.
4. He will 'tread out the winepress of Almighty God's fierce retribution.' This links this prophecy to the prophecies in Joel 4:13 and Isaiah 63:3.

The Day of the Lord Draws Closer

5. 'Then I saw the beast, with all the kings of the earth and their armies, gathered together to fight the Rider and his army.' They are gathered together at Armageddon (Revelation 16:16). These details confirm the prophecies in Ezekiel 38 and 39 and others, that the warfare will take place in Israel.
6. And 'all the birds glutted themselves with their flesh' (19:21, see also 19:17,18). These references to the feast of the birds of prey link the text with Ezekiel 39:17-20 and to Jesus' references to vultures being gathered around carcasses.
7. 'And the beast was taken, and with him the false prophet ... and both were cast alive into the lake of burning fire and sulphur' (19:20). This confirms the prophecy in 2 Thessalonians 2:8, that the Lord will destroy the man of iniquity with the breath of his mouth on the Day of his coming.

Take this account of the Rider and his armies in combination with the other six prophecies of the Day of the Lord in the Book of Revelation, and we have a coherent description of what will happen, fully consistent with all the earlier prophecies.

What follows in Chapter 20 is likewise consistent with the earlier prophecies. Satan is bound with 'an enormous chain' (20:1), being the chain formed by the prayers of the saints, and is locked up in the Abyss for a thousand years. In Ezekiel 38 and 39, the key result of the Day of the Lord will be that both Israel and the Gentile world will know, from that day forward and forever, who their true Messiah is, that he is Christ the Lord (Ezekiel 38:23, 39:7, 22, 27-29), and they will be willingly subject to him.

In Revelation 20, this conversion of the nations beginning with Israel finds expression in the prophecy of the thousand year reign of Christ and his saints.

> I saw the souls of those who had been beheaded for the witness of Jesus and for the word of God, and those who refused to worship the beast or his statue and who refused to accept his mark on their foreheads or on their hands; they lived and reigned with Christ for a thousand years.   - Revelation 20:4

Chapter 20 then provides a further account of conflict, occurring immediately after the end of the thousand year reign of Christ and his saints, and immediately before the Final Judgment and the introduction of the new heaven and the new earth. The first mention of Gog and Magog in the Book of Revelation occurs in this account (20:8). This is the seventh of the series of descriptions of the Day of the Lord, which we discussed earlier.

SIGNS OF THE TIMES

Is the Day of the Lord imminent? Is it likely to happen in our lifetimes? Does the flood of filth thrown forth by our media mean that God's patience with us is all but run out? Does the stranglehold of antichristian governments over so many of the nations of the earth mean that divine intervention is at hand? Is the sudden triumph of homosexual politics in so many parts of the world a sign that Babylon is about to go up in smoke?

Or has God found the ten just men in the cities of our modern world to justify a stay of execution? Have the prayers and the sufferings of the saints been sufficient to defer the Day for some time longer?

These questions are impossible to answer. We can see which way the wind is blowing. We can see events moving swiftly toward disaster. We can see the Day looming. But we cannot know the date or the hour.

Fr Gobbi, the founder of the Marian Movement of Priests, heard Mary say this to him:

"I am telling you the dangers through which you are going, the imminent threats, the extent of the evils which could happen to you, only because these evils can yet be avoided by you, the dangers can be evaded, the plan of God's justice can always be changed by the force of his merciful love. Also, remember that everything, at any moment, may be changed by the force of your prayer and your reparative penance." - To the Priests, Our Lady's Beloved Sons, Title 282

Our prayer is much more powerful than we think. It has the power to change the course of history.

Does this mean that our prayer can cause biblical prophesies not to be fulfilled?

This is a difficult one. There are instances in Scripture of the word of God coming as a warning, but when the hearers repented, the warning didn't take effect, or its fulfillment was deferred. Jonah prophesied that Nineveh would be destroyed within forty days, but when the Ninevites repented in sackcloth with fasting, God relented and the destruction was avoided. Elijah prophesied the destruction of the house of Ahab, but when Ahab did public penance, the Lord declared that he would not bring down the disaster in the lifetime of Ahab, but in the lifetime of his son (2 Kings 21:29).

God never closes his ears to entreaty. Repentance gains his attention. His warnings are meant to wake us up so we can turn to him and be saved. As Mary goes on to say in the same title of Fr Gobbi's account:

> "Do not say therefore, 'How much of what you predicted to us has not come true!' Instead, give thanks with me to the Heavenly Father because in response to your prayer and consecration, on account of your suffering and of the immense suffering of so many of my poor children, again He alters the period of justice, to permit his great mercy to come to flower."

God changes his mind in response to our prayer. When he sees our faith in him in spite of our temptation to doubt, he alters his plan. Persistent faith will bear fruit, and to give it time to do so, he defers the day of reckoning.

On the other hand, biblical prophesy is fulfilled. Nineveh's empire did eventually collapse. The house of Ahab was destroyed in the following generation. Jesus, when the day of his sacrifice was drawing near, did not seek to defer it. Everything he did at that time, he did in order that the scriptures might be fulfilled.

> "Do you think I cannot pray to my Father, who would straightaway send me twelve legions of angels? But then how would the scriptures be fulfilled that say this is how it must be?"
>
> - Matthew 26:53,54

What is even more difficult to understand, he took no steps to lead Judas Iscariot to repentance, and for the same reason. He said this while praying to the Father:

> "Those whom you gave me I have kept, and none of them is lost except the son of perdition, that the Scripture might be fulfilled." - John 17:12

We cannot stop the Day of the Lord from happening. To attempt that would be to ignore the prophecies in Scripture. What we can do is greatly ameliorate its impacts for ourselves, for our church communities, and for our nations. The Day of the Lord will take place. Who will fall, who will survive, who will go to perdition, who will be saved – none of this has been fixed by some malevolent fate. No, even as he prophesied the disaster, the prophet Joel immediately held out the remedy, available to all without exception:

> The sun will be turned to darkness,
> and the moon into blood,
> before the Day comes,
> that great and terrible Day;
> All who call on the name of the Lord will be saved.
> - Joel 3:4,5

It looks like an anomaly. Even in the midst of the great and terrible Day, 'All who call on the name of the Lord will be saved.' Joel is here announcing the purpose of the Day, which is salvation and not destruction.

In everything God does with us his people, he is seeking to prosper us and not to harm us. There is no place for fatalism. Fatalism is the opposite of what the Bible tells us.

> But you brothers, do not live in the dark, for that Day to overtake you like a thief ... God destined us not for his retribution, but to win salvation through Our Lord Jesus Christ.   - 1 Thessalonians 5:4-9

So the Day is coming, but we are not fated to be swept away in it. We are called to be delivered from it.

How soon will it arrive? Will it be in our lifetimes?

The time and date is not given to us. We must never forget that. If we pretend we can predict the date of his coming we are fooling ourselves and we are at risk of going astray.

Our task is given to us by Our Lord. He commissions us to go out and spread his kingdom. We are to proclaim his kingship and to welcome all peoples into his kingdom. The gospel is to be proclaimed throughout the entire world before the end will come.

As long as we don't lose sight of that, and as long as we do not claim special knowledge on the subject, there is nothing wrong with having a view as to whether the Day will come in our lifetimes or whether it will happen further in the future. Jesus, after all, lamented that the Pharisees and Sadducees were able to predict the weather from the color of the sky, 'but you cannot read the signs of the times' (Matthew 16:3).

The trends are established. The growth in lawlessness; the falling away from love; the spread of homosexual practice and its justification in laws and in the education of the young; the explosion in the persecution of Christians; the spread of anti-Semitism and the growing threats against the integrity of Israel and Jerusalem as the land and city given by God to his people the Jews; the corruption of faith through the flow of filth coming from the world's media: the falling away of Christians into apostasy; these all point clearly toward the coming of the Day of retribution.

But are we at the point where the man of iniquity is about to appear, when he will abolish the daily sacrifice for a time, and install the abomination of desolation, and pollute the sanctuary of God, and mouth his blasphemies and flaunt the ludicrous claim that he himself is God?

I don't think we are at that point, but we are moving toward it. The trends have been set in motion; we are witnessing the early signs of what is to come; but I don't think it will come in our lifetimes. In Title 407 of his book, Fr Gobbi reports Mary as dividing the history of the activities of Antichrist into three main periods, each lasting 666 years, in line with the name of the beast.

The first of those three periods began around 666 a.d. with the founding of the religion of Islam. The second began around 1332 with the beginning of rationalistic approaches to the search for truth which would split the church and ultimately destroy faith in the word of God. Regarding the third period, the 666 years beginning around 1998, Fr Gobbi reports Mary as saying this:

"In this period of history Freemasonry ... will succeed in its great design: that of setting up an idol to put in the place of Christ and of his Church, a false christ and a false church. Consequently, the statue built in honor of the first beast, to be adored by all the inhabitants of the earth and which will seal with its mark all those who wish to buy or sell, is that of the Antichrist. You have thus arrived at the peak of the purification, of the great tribulation and of the apostasy. The apostasy will then be generalized because almost all will follow the false christ. Then the door will be open for the appearance of the man or the very person of the Antichrist."

- To the Priests, Our Lady's Beloved Sons, Title 407

This passage, though it is taken from an account of private revelations and so does not carry the same authority as Scripture or defined Church teaching, nevertheless provides a highly credible account of how things are building up in the church and in the world of recent times.

If Fr Gobbi has heard Mary accurately, it tells us that the Day of the Lord, which will follow from the appearance of the Antichrist, is still centuries away. It will happen sometime in the period of 666 years beginning around 1998. As it will be the climactic event bringing to a halt the process of corruption building up during this period, it is reasonable to suppose that it will happen closer to the end of this period than to the beginning.

For what it is worth – and we are only speaking of very uncertain guesses here – I feel that the timescale that can be derived from this passage gives us about the closest idea of the true timescale that we can have. It means, again if Fr Gobbi has heard Mary correctly, that a few decades ago, a six and a half century period began in which the creeping power of Freemasonry started to gather momentum.

When, over the coming centuries (we don't know how many) the forces of Antichrist succeed in turning all the peoples of the earth to the service of the beast and his agenda, the stage will finally be set for the horrifying events preceding the Day of the Lord: the appearance of the Antichrist; the abolition of the Mass; the installation of the abomination of desolation; then the vast military march into Israel to take control of the holy city Jerusalem.

At that point, when all seems utterly lost, when the infernal dragon appears to be in total control of the world, the Warrior-Messiah will intervene on behalf of his people, and the eyes of all, beginning with Israel, will be opened, the truth will at last dawn, and all the peoples of the world will find the deepest relief in turning in repentance and conversion to their only Savior.

They will look on the one whom they have pierced and know at last that in him lies their only hope. The nations of the world will at long last recognize their Savior and will not be deluded again for a very long time, a thousand years. The earth will at long last be filled with the knowledge of the only true God as the waters cover the sea.

THE DIFFERENCE

In the days of Rehoboam king of Judah, the armies of Judah were defeated by the army of Shishak king of Egypt. The prophet Shemaiah prophesied that the reason for their defeat was their abandonment of Yahweh to serve other gods. Rehoboam and his people repented and returned to the worship of Yahweh, and Yahweh gave them a measure of relief.

> When Yahweh saw that they had humbled themselves, the word of Yahweh came to Shemaiah as follows: "They have humbled themselves. I will not destroy them but will grant them some degree of deliverance. My retribution will not be poured out on Jerusalem by means of Shishak; they are nonetheless to become his servants so that they may learn the difference between serving me and serving the kings of other nations." - 2 Chronicles 12:7,8

This scripture provides us with the template for all of our experience on this earth. Throughout our lives, in so many circumstances and so many ways, God is teaching us the difference between the misery of serving the powers of hell, and the joy of serving the Lord. The two are a lot more different than chalk and cheese. They are the difference between everlasting life and everlasting death.

The chief effect of the Day of the Lord will be that we will know this difference. The terrifying events of the Day will impress it so clearly on the minds of the peoples of the earth that they will not forget it again for a thousand years.

The chief root of confusion and evil in the world we are living in is that we have lost awareness of this difference. We treat antichristian religion as if it were equivalent to faith in Christ. We treat sin as if it were virtue. We speak of evil as if it were good. We treat demonic gods as if they could rival the living and true God for our attention.

This confusion of spirits is the root spiritual sickness. The Day of the Lord will be the remedy.

If we can understand this, and turn to Christ and his Church for healing, we can prepare for the Day of the Lord so as to avoid its dire effects.

Every time we take to honoring other gods, we cut ourselves off from the living and true God, and we draw horrific curses on ourselves, curses first pronounced by the word of God in very many texts of the Bible, and confirmed many times by the authoritative declarations of the Church.

The idea that antichristian religions are good never comes from the Holy Spirit. The Holy Spirit always gives testimony to Jesus, the true manifestation of God, and never to any spirits hostile to Jesus. The idea that antichristian religions are good is at the center of the teachings of Freemasonry.

We need to remain clear on this and never allow ourselves to be confused about it: The Holy Spirit always testifies to Jesus, and will never testify to any spirit refusing to confess Jesus for who he truly is. Scripture defines the true spirit of prophecy, prophecy inspired by the Holy Spirit, in exactly these terms:

> The testimony of Jesus is the spirit of prophecy.
>
> - Revelation 19:10

Amen. The whole of the Old Testament testifies to Jesus. The whole of the New Testament testifies to Jesus. The Holy Spirit testifies to Jesus. The church testifies to Jesus. All good religion testifies to Jesus. If religion does not confess Jesus for who he is, it is not good religion, and the spirit of prophecy is not in it.

What is the problem with praising the religions that do not confess Christ?

The problem is that these other religions are the work of sinister spirits, spirits hostile to faith in Christ, and when we praise such spirits we are aligning ourselves spiritually with them; we are opening a door for them to enter and wreak the most terrible havoc in our souls. The consequences of doing this are extremely serious, because where demons are, Christ and his grace cannot be. When we accept wicked spirits into our souls we drive out the grace of God given to us in Christ; we become incapable of resisting temptation; we are thus driven to all manner of sins and shameless activities;

we become prone to sickness of mind and body; we are at serious risk of self destruction through suicide.

How do we know that the spirits that do not confess Christ are wicked spirits? Might we not be speaking simply of blameless ignorance of Christ among the devotees of false religions? Should we not excuse people instead of condemning them? Should we not admit that they are acting in invincible ignorance?

We are not condemning individual humans here. Judgment belongs to God, not to us. But God has not commissioned us to leave people in their ignorance of the truth about Christ. He has commissioned us to go boldly into the whole world and proclaim Christ as the truth.

Spirits who, for centuries, even for millennia, lead people to reject faith in Christ, could not possibly be good spirits. They demonstrate by their hostility to Christ that they are sinister spirits.

When sinister spirits gain a foothold among God's people, the Holy Spirit leaves, and God's people are left with the horrible fruits that sinister spirits always bring, fruits of destruction on all levels, spiritual, emotional, physical, moral, social, financial, occupational ...

Spirits can only give us what they have. Because what sinister spirits have is utter destruction, utter destruction is all they can give us. And utter destruction is what they do give us when we align ourselves with them by praising them, so driving the Holy Spirit away from us.

Bear in mind that the Bible commands us to test the spirits. It commands us not to judge our fellow humans, it is true; it also commands us to test the spirits to see if they are of God.

That these spirits are hostile to God himself was stated explicitly by Jesus when he said, "He who rejects me rejects the one who sent me" (Luke 10:16).

You cannot mix faith in Christ with the praise of the spirits hostile to him.

Who is the liar but the one who denies that Jesus is the Christ? This is the Antichrist, who denies both the Father and the Son. Whoever denies the Son cannot have the Father either. Whoever confesses the

> Son has the Father too. Let what you heard in the beginning remain in you. - 1 John 2:22-24

The apostle John goes on to make this principle the foundation of the test of spirits. We are commanded to apply this test to discern which spirits are of God, and which spirits are of the devil. The good spirits confess Jesus for who he is. The sinister spirits do not confess Jesus for who he is (1 John 4:1-4). That is how we know the difference.

Praise, as we've noted earlier, is a sacrifice. It involves us in turning our attention off ourselves and giving it to the object of our praise. If we praise the living and true God and his Christ, we are offering our sacrifice to him and we will receive powerful blessings as a result. If we offer our sacrifice of praise to occult spirits, the consequences will be horrific beyond description.

> Through Christ, let us offer to God the continual sacrifice of praise, the fruit of the lips of those who confess his name. - Hebrews 13:15

Does Scripture have anything to say about those who offer their sacrifice of praise not to the God of Israel who came among us in Christ, but to other gods? It does.

> He who sacrifices to other gods will be placed under the curse of destruction.　　　- Exodus 22:19

It is very instructive to take a look at what goes wrong when we Christians praise false religion, and how embarrassing the consequences are. It brings us once again face to face with the message God has been giving his people from the beginning, the message that appears on every page of Scripture because we need to learn it, again, and again, and again.

Worship the true God alone, the one who took flesh in Christ, and you will be blessed in all things and in all events and at all times. Turn aside to other gods, and all the curses set out in Deuteronomy 28, and elsewhere in Scripture, will come upon you and overtake you.

And you will have no idea what is going on, why so many and such great disasters have overtaken you, until he leads you into the wilderness and speaks to your heart, and you learn once again to call him by his name alone, and to stop calling him by the names of the false and demonic gods who have nothing to offer except destruction.

There is something mysterious in our capacity to honor other gods, reap horrible consequences by so doing, and yet have no clue as to the link between the abominable cause and the horrible effect. The demons thrive on secrecy. It is the air they breathe. Once their deeds are brought into the Light, they are forced to flee. But as long as they can keep us from noticing, as long as they can hide from us the causal link between the root and the fruit, they can continue to work their destruction in us.

It normally takes some kind of deliverance ministry to wake us up to what has happened. Then we can kick ourselves for missing the message that Scripture gives us on every page, as we move forward to shake off the horrible influences identified and walk in a deeper knowledge and a greater joy than ever before, knowing that all our blessings, without exception, come from the Lord of glory by the Blood he shed for us on the Cross.

There is no joy like the joy of waking up and driving the wicked spirits far from us in the power given to us by our Savior. If we experience this, we get some inkling of what it will be like after the Day of the Lord, when the entire earth, having come through great deception and great tribulation followed by great revelation, will be filled with the knowledge of the only living and true God as the waters cover the sea.

WHAT WILL IT LOOK LIKE AFTER THE DAY?

We will take a look here at what some of the scriptures say about the features of the world in the centuries following the terrible traumas of the Day. We will then make some more general comments on what the world will look like in that era.

1. The nation of Israel will know who the true God is, that he is the one who took flesh in Christ, and this knowledge will not leave them. This will be the primary effect of the Day, the root blessing from which all the other blessings will come upon the world. The repetitions throughout the Book of Ezekiel – 'And then you will know that I am the Lord,' – there are more than fifty of them, tell us of a desire deep in the heart of God that his Christ will be recognized by his own people. They will not see his face again until this happens; when it does happen, it will be 'nothing less than life from the dead,' not only for Israel, but for all the nations of the earth.

2. The conversion of Israel to faith in Christ will bring all of those Gentile nations which had come against Israel to faith in Christ as well. They will not be deceived by idolatry again, after the dragon has been chained and locked into the Abyss. 'For the earth will be filled with the knowledge of God as the waters cover the sea.' We've also seen this prophecy in Ezekiel 38:23 and 39:7,22,28,29.

3. When that time comes, the Lord himself will rejoice and sing and dance over his people Israel, as we've seen in Zephaniah 3:18 ('he will dance with shouts of joy for you, as on a day of festival').

4. The Name of the Lord will be one. He will not be called by the names of false gods. We've seen from the other prophecies that this Name is the Name of Jesus the Christ. 'When that Day comes, there will be one Lord, and his Name one' (Zechariah 14:9).

> Therefore my people will know my Name; therefore they will know when that Day comes that it is I saying, 'Here I am!'   - Isaiah 52:6

All the peoples of the world, having experienced the horrors of being trapped into honoring demonic spirits, will be so relieved to escape from them that they will be filled with gratitude to the true God for giving them the escape route by letting them know the Holy Name of their Savior. They will honor his Name with a greater fervor than has ever been known before.

5. A time of great healing will follow the Day of the Lord.

> At that time I will undo all that afflicted you;
> when that time comes,
> I will rescue the lame,
> and gather the strays,
> and I will win them praise and renown
> in every land where they have been put to shame.
>   - Zephaniah 3:19

The moonlight will be bright as sunlight,
and sunlight will be seven times brighter,
like the light of seven days in one,
on the Day Yahweh dresses his people's wound,
and heals the scars of their blows.

- Isaiah 30:26

I will look for the lost one,
bring back the stray,
bandage the injured,
and strengthen the sick.
I will watch over the fat and healthy.
I will be a true shepherd to them.

- Ezekiel 34:16

6. The era after the Day of the Lord will be a time of great peace in the world. That peace will rest on the only foundation we can truly rely on, the knowledge of God which is in Christ. This knowledge will be everywhere. It will be shared throughout all the nations of the earth.

> The wolf will lie down with the lamb,
> and the leopard will lie down with the kid;
> the calf, the young lion, and the fatling together,
> and a little boy will lead them ...
> no hurt, no harm will be done
> on all my holy mountain,
> for the earth will be full of the knowledge of Yahweh
> as the waters cover the sea.
>
> - Isaiah 11:6-9

7. It will be a time of purification. Idolatry and occult practice of all kinds will be driven out, and the peoples will know the importance of and will observe personal purity. Sexual activity will be respected only between married partners with openness to procreation, and people everywhere will instinctively shrink from all forms of unfaithfulness, adultery and fornication, recognizing them immediately and naturally for the horrible things they are. All sexual uncleanness will be recognized as sinful, immediately and without any awkwardness. Confusion of spirits will be gone.

Corrosive entertainments will be no more. Pornography will have been consigned to sordid history.

> When that Day comes, Yahweh declares, I will cut off the names of the idols from the land, and they will be remembered no more. I will also rid the land of the prophets and of the spirit of impurity.
> - Zechariah 13:2

> You will hold unclean the silverplating of your idols, and the goldplating of your images. You will throw them away like the polluted things they are, shouting after them, 'Get thee hence!' - Isaiah 30:22

8. Christ and his followers will reign throughout the earth. This is clear in the prophecies in both the Old and New Testaments. The myth of the 'separation of church and state,' by which the governments of the age in which we live have set themselves up as enemies of the wisdom of God and champions of the horrible kingdom of Antichrist, all of this will have disappeared after the Day of the Lord, recognized for the ugly

deception it has always been. There will be a wholly new knowledge of the truth of Scripture: 'There is no wisdom, nor understanding, nor counsel, against the Lord (Proverbs 21:30).

This was the horn I had watched making war on the holy ones and proving the stronger, until the coming of the One most Venerable who gave judgment in favor of the holy ones of the Most High, when the time came for the holy ones to assume kingship.
- Daniel 7:21,22

But the court will sit, and he *(Antichrist)* will be stripped of his royal authority, which will be finally destroyed and reduced to nothing. And kingship and rule and the splendors of all the kingdoms under heaven will be given to the people of the holy ones of the Most High, whose royal power is an eternal power, whom every empire will serve and obey.
- Daniel 7:26,27

> And I saw thrones, and they sat upon them, and judgment was given to them: and I saw the souls of those who were beheaded for the witness of Jesus, and for the word of God, and who had not worshipped the beast, nor his image, nor had they received his mark on their foreheads or in their hands; and they lived and reigned with Christ a thousand years.   - Revelation 20:4

9. The Church's liturgical celebrations will be more glorious, more pure, more full voiced, more filled with the mysterious joy of heaven than they will ever have been before. A wholly new appreciation of the Eucharist will be the mainspring of the church's life in the long period following the Day of the Lord. Everything the Church will do will be the work of the Eucharist, and the Eucharistic Christ will receive the glory for it.

    I infer these things from the prophecies in Daniel and the gospels which center on the abolition of the Mass and the installation of the abomination of desolation in its place. If these horrors form the pinnacle of Satan's purpose in leading all the peoples of the world astray, it follows that the restoration of the recognition of the Eucharist throughout the church will be the central outcome of the Day of the Lord.

10. There will be a passionate desire for the word of God among the peoples of the earth after the Day of the Lord. His appearing on the Day will dispel all thoughts of idolatry and syncretistic practice. People will kick themselves so hard for allowing neglect of the word of God to make them sitting targets of their spiritual enemies who led them astray by their flood of false words, that from then on they will desire nothing more than to live by every word that proceeds out of the mouth of God.

11. There will be an end of divisions and hostilities in the church. Manufactured opposition between the Eucharist and the word of God will be seen through for the destructive deception it is, and there will be a joyful acceptance of each other's gifts among all parts of the church.

12. Believers will walk in the fear of the Lord, which brings immense blessings as we know from Scripture. They will be fully alive to the difference between heaven and hell, and will have a highly developed sensitivity to which actions lead toward one, and which lead toward the other. They will know, from their knowledge of the Day, the indescribable joy that radiates wherever Christ is held in honor. They will know that heaven can only exist where Christ is.

And they will know the indescribable horror of dwelling where Satan dwells. The utterly indescribable horror of direct spirit to spirit contact with millions of venomous and sneering demons headed by the Antichrist in hell is the inverse of the joy of spiritual contact with Christ in the Communion of Saints in heaven. Just as no words could come close to describing the joy of heaven, no words could possibly describe the horrors of hell either. Christians in the long era following the Day of the Lord will be keenly aware of the difference.

13. Believers in the Name will have an unprecedented gift for discerning the plan that God conceived for their lives from his eternity. 'Your old men shall see visions, and your young men shall dream dreams' (Joel 3:1). The ability to discern the call we have received from God is one of the results of the fear of the Lord.

> If anyone fears the Lord,
> he will show him the path he should choose.
> - Psalm 25:12

The fruits that this gift will bring to individuals, to the church and to the world, are hard to imagine now. The joy of discovering the call God has placed on our lives is impossible to imagine. You can only experience it.

God's plan for each of us is unique. When we discern it we realize just how intimately and completely he understands us. Discerning and following his plan for us binds us intimately to him, and this is the reason for the joy it brings us. This is 'the white stone, with a new name written on it, known only to the one who receives it' (Revelation 2:17). And the result of individuals discerning and following the unique call God has given them is to change the course of history.

14. We don't know what the population of the world will be in future eras, but it would not surprise me to find that the great majority of all humans will live in the thousand years of the reign of Christ and his saints. It would be wholly in keeping with what we know of the generosity of God to place most humans in the era which he himself has made clean, so they can have the benefit of his mighty works. The door is narrow and the way is straight, it is true, but don't forget that the number of the saved is 'a vast number that no man could count' (Revelation 7:9).

It is difficult for us to imagine what a radically different future might look like, because it is difficult for us to have a critical perspective on the world we currently inhabit, the world in which we have perhaps learned to feel all too comfortable. The ideas underpinning the way of life of the people around us tend to gain a foothold in our minds without our being clearly aware of how it happens, and it can be close to impossible to kick off the faulty foundations.

It is not impossible, however. Our minds are not fated to remain forever imprisoned in someone else's thought structures. When God comes to our help we can easily break free. The word of God is very powerful and it releases us from all bonds.

Sometimes humor is the best way to gain an objective perspective on where we have gone wrong. In Psalm 2, God describes himself as laughing at the ruling persons and the ruling ideas governing the world in this period of history, before the Day of the Lord. We presume these ruling ideas are axiomatic truths, fixed and unchallengeable. We need to wake up and realize that God, who is Truth itself, is laughing them to scorn.

It is worth reading Psalm 2 with the purpose of gaining God's understanding on the ideas and conceptions underpinning the confused and wicked civilization we are living in. The psalm opens with a scene of 'uproar' across all the nations on earth.

> Why this uproar among the nations,
>
> this impotent muttering of the peoples?
>
> Kings of the earth take up position,
>
> and the rulers take counsel together
>
> against the Lord and his anointed, saying,
>
> 'Now let us break their fetters!
>
> Now let us cast off their bonds!'
>
> - Psalm 2:1-3

The war preparations in question are for the conflict on the Great Day. The uproar among the nations against the so called 'bonds' which God's commandments place on us looks very familiar. For a long time now the nations have been provoking God to his face, pushing back further and further against his commandments. It will reach the point of outright war, against Israel, against Jerusalem, and against the Church which upholds God's word and his commandments.

How does God our Father respond to this? Is he upset about it? Is he disheartened by it? Is he threatened by it? No, he laughs at it. He makes a mockery of it.

> He who sits in the heavens laughs,
> Yahweh makes a mockery of them.
>
> \- Psalm 2:4

Then he speaks in anger. They haven't been listening. They have ignored his word. He tells them that the king has already been anointed and enthroned on Zion, his holy mountain. This is a prophecy of the Day of the Lord, which will strike terror in the nations at a time they least expect, causing them to realize in an instant who the true king is, and how foolish they have been in resisting him.

> Then he will speak in his wrath,
> in his rage he will strike them with terror:
> 'It is I who have set my king
> on Zion, my holy mountain.'
>
> \- Psalm 2:5,6

Next, the Son speaks of the plan which the Holy Trinity had conceived originally, from his eternity, before anything had been created.

> I will proclaim the decree of Yahweh:
> he said to me, 'You are my Son,
> today I have fathered you.'
> - Psalm 2:7

The part in quotes is a key text, repeated a number of times at critical points in Scripture. These are the words used by the Holy Spirit at the baptism of Jesus (Luke 3:22). Paul cited them in his address to the Jews (Acts 13:33). They are cited in Hebrews 1:5 and 5:5. They are presented in slightly different terms in Psalm 110:3.

> 'Ask of me and I will give you the nations as your inheritance,
> the farthest parts of the earth as your possession.
> With a rod of iron you will break them,
> you will dash them to pieces like a potter's vessel.
> - Psalm 2:8,9

This is grim language about the destruction that will take place on the Day of the Lord. Against all expectation, it will be the Day on which the kingship of Christ is established in every part of the earth.

The last three verses give compassionate counsel to the rulers of the earth and to their peoples, telling them how to be well prepared for the terrifying events to come. This advice is addressed to the rulers and peoples of all ages.

> 'So now, you kings,
> come to your senses,
> you rulers of the earth,
> receive your instruction.
> Serve the Lord with fear,
> and rejoice with trembling.
> Kiss his feet, lest he be angry,
> and your way come to nothing,
> for his fury flares up in a moment.
> Blessed are all they that put their trust in him.'
> - Psalm 2:10-12

There is no other way. Trust in the true God, the one who took flesh in Christ, because this is the only way out of the destruction that will take place on the Day of the Lord.

The time is coming when it will be plain to everyone how shallow were the ideas that got so deeply implanted in the minds of this age we are living in.

The time is coming when homosexual politics and everything to do with the sin against nature will be recognized as carrying the abominable stench it always had. In the era following the Day of the Lord, people will look back and find it almost impossible to believe that whole nations could ever have become so obstinate and so confused as they became before the Day on this issue.

The time is coming when people will weep over the loss of those who could have brought great gifts into our world, but who were sacrificed to our convenience in the holocaust of abortion.

The time is coming when parents will no longer hand over our children to educators to be propagandized with every form of confusion and evil, and to have the only source of true power, which is faith in Christ, robbed from them and replaced with a poisonous mix of demon inspired beliefs. All of this will be seen for the monstrous fraud it really is.

The time is coming when everyone will hold in derision the idea that the word of God only has application in the so called 'private' sphere and can have no application in public, political and professional life because these spheres have been taken over by antichristian forces.

A key difference between our world and the world that will emerge following the Day of the Lord, is that after the Day, all the nations of the earth will know the difference between blessing and curse. They will know where all blessings come from. They will know that blessings can only come in the name of the Lord, the Christ. And they will know the source of every curse. They will know that all those spirits hostile to Christ have nothing to offer except destruction.

When the Day of the Lord has woken us up, all these things will be clear to us. We will not forget them. The events of the Day of the Lord, terrifying to those who resist him, filled with the hope of the glorious new era to those who rejoice in him, will be recorded in complete visual detail and will be remembered by all succeeding generations.

In the meantime, before the Day of the Lord comes, there is nothing to prevent God's people, individual believers, nations, church communities, from learning the lessons in advance, and so finding protection from the wrath to come. It has all been prophesied many times in Scripture so that we can receive all the knowledge we need to prepare for it.

Those last, comforting, strengthening, revealing lines of Psalm 2 are not only addressed by the psalmist to rulers and peoples in the distant future. They are addressed to rulers and peoples now, in every age and in every place. 'So <u>now</u>, you kings, come to your senses.' The psalmist was addressing the peoples of his time and of every time, throughout the entire earth. 'Blessed <u>are</u> all those who put their trust in him.' It doesn't say, Blessed will be … but, 'Blessed are …' We are called to act on these words now.

The Day of the Lord Draws Closer

We do not need to wait for the Day of the Lord to overtake us like a thief. We are urged to be prepared. We are invited to take the winning side before the terrible conflict is upon us. We are warned to stay alert and not to lose the grace of God as we wait for what seems like a very long time.

> "Stay awake therefore, for you don't know when the master of the house will come, at evening, at midnight, at cockcrow, or in the morning, lest he come suddenly and find you asleep. What I say to you I say to all: Stay awake!"   - Mark 13:35-37

It is not easy to stay prepared as we live through the times of tribulation, when the nations of the earth are still walking in so much confusion. And it will get much worse before the Day comes. To stay awake, to keep our robes clean, to remain in the grace of God through such times, we need all the help we can get.

Chapter 12 of Revelation shows the Son being taken up to heaven while his Mother remains on earth to do battle with the dragon. Consecration to the Mother of

God is the most powerful way to remain close to Christ through the ordeal. 'The Lord is with you,' the angel Gabriel said to her (Luke 1:28). If we find it hard to stay close to him, we can easily do so by staying close to the one he is close to, the one who has the dragon under her feet, the one appointed by the Father to remain with us while her Son seems to be so far away, while it takes him so long to appear.

Where Mary is Queen, Jesus is King.

Amen. Come, Lord Jesus, dispel the confusion, and let every nation on earth be submitted to your kingship, where we find the only joy, the only peace, now and to ages unending. Amen.

www.ingramcontent.com/pod-product-compliance
Lightning Source LLC
Chambersburg PA
CBHW051645040426
42446CB00009B/990